PLOTINUS

ENNEAD I.8

THE *ENNEADS* OF PLOTINUS

With Philosophical Commentaries

Series Editors: John M. Dillon, Trinity College, Dublin
and Andrew Smith, University College, Dublin

Also Available:

I.1: *What Is the Living Thing? What Is Man?* by Gerard O'Daly
I.5: *On Whether Well-Being Increases with Time* by Danielle A. Layne
I.6: *On Beauty* by Andrew Smith
II.4: *On Matter* by Anthony A. Long
II.5: *On What Is Potentially and What Actually* by Cinzia Arruzza
II.9: *Against the Gnostics* by Sebastian Ramon Philipp Gertz
III.4: *On Our Allotted Guardian Spirit* by Wiebke-Marie Stock
IV.3–4.29: *Problems Concerning the Soul* by John M. Dillon & H. J. Blumenthal
IV.4.30–45 & IV.5: *Problems Concerning the Soul* by Gary Gurtler
IV.7: *On the Immortality of the Soul* by Barrie Fleet
IV.8: *On the Descent of the Soul Into Bodies* by Barrie Fleet
V.1: *On the Three Primary Levels of Reality* by Eric D. Perl
V.5: *That the Intelligibles are not External to Intellect, and on the Good* by Lloyd P. Gerson
V.8: *On Intelligible Beauty* by Andrew Smith
VI.4 & VI.5: *On the Presence of Being, One and the Same, Everywhere as a Whole* by Eyjólfur Emilsson & Steven Strange
VI.8: *On the Voluntary and on the Free Will of the One* by Kevin Corrigan and John D. Turner
VI.9: *On the Good or the One* by Stephen R. L. Clark

Forthcoming:

I.2: *On Virtues* by Suzanne Stern-Gillet
I.3: *On Dialectic* by Pauliina Remes
I.4: *On Well-Being* by Kieran McGroarty
I.9: *On Going Out of the Body* by Suzanne Stern-Gilet
II.1: *On the Heavens* by Andrew Smith
II.6: *On Substance, or On Quality* by Damien Caluori
II.7: *On Complete Blending* by Robert Goulding
II.8: *On Sight* by Robert Goulding
III.5: *On Love* by Sara Magrin
III.6: *On Impassibility* by Eleni Perdikouri
III.7: *On Eternity and Time* by László Bene
III.8: *On Nature and Contemplation* by George Karamanolis
IV.6: *On Sense-Perception and Memory* by Peter Lautner
IV.9: *On Whether All Souls are One* by Eyjólfur Emilsson
V.2, **V.4**, and **V.6**: *On the One and Intellect* by Eleni Perdikouri
V.3: *On the Knowing Hypostases* by Marie-Élise Zovko
V.9: *On Intellect, Ideas, and Being* by Matthias Vorwerk
VI.1–2: *On the Genera of Being (I+II)* by Damien Caluori & Regina Füchslin
VI.3: *On the Genera of Being (III)* by Riccardo Chiaradonna
VI.7: *The Forms and the Good* by Nicholas Banner

PLOTINUS
ENNEAD I.8

On the Nature and Source of Evil

Translation with an Introduction and Commentary

ANNE SHEPPARD

PARMENIDES
PUBLISHING

Las Vegas | Zurich | Athens

PARMENIDES PUBLISHING
Las Vegas | Zurich | Athens

This edition published in 2025 by Parmenides Publishing
in the United States of America

ISBN soft cover: 979-8-9883201-2-8
ISBN e-Book: 979-8-9883201-3-5

Library of Congress Cataloging-in-Publication Data

Names: Plotinus, author. | Sheppard, Anne D. R., translator, writer of added commentary.
Title: Ennead, I.8, On the nature and source of evil / translation with an Introduction and commentary Anne Sheppard.
Other titles: Enneads. I, 8. English | On the nature and source of evil
Description: 1st. | Las Vegas : Parmenides Publishing, [2025] | Series: The Enneads of Plotinus with philosophical commentaries | Includes bibliographical references and index. | Summary: "In Ennead I.8 Plotinus argues that evil is not intrinsic to the soul; the treatise includes an account of the metaphysical status of matter and a nuanced presentation of the way in which matter and the soul can together be responsible for moral evil"-- Provided by publisher.
Identifiers: LCCN 2024049659 (print) | LCCN 2024049660 (ebook) | ISBN 9798988320128 (paperback) | ISBN 9798988320135 (ebook)
Subjects: LCSH: Neoplatonism--Early works to 1800. | Good and evil--Early works to 1800. | Plotinus. Enneads. I, 8.
Classification: LCC B693.E52 E5 2025 (print) | LCC B693.E52 (ebook) | DDC 186/.4--dc23/eng/20241106
LC record available at https://lccn.loc.gov/2024049659
LC ebook record available at https://lccn.loc.gov/2024049660

Typeset in Warnock and Futura by M Rules, London, UK
Printed digitally by Integrated Books International (IBI), Chicago, IL

www.parmenides.com

Contents

Introduction to the Series With a Brief Outline of the Life and Thought of Plotinus (205–270 CE)

PLOTINUS WAS BORN IN 205 CE in Egypt of Greek-speaking parents. He attended the philosophical schools in Alexandria where he would have studied Plato (427–347 BCE), Aristotle (384–322 BCE), the Stoics and Epicureans as well as other Greek philosophical traditions. He began his serious philosophical education, however, relatively late in life, at the age of twenty-seven and was deeply impressed by the Platonist Ammonius Saccas about whom we, unfortunately, know very little, but with whom Plotinus studied for some eleven years. Even our knowledge of Plotinus' life is limited to what we can glean from Porphyry's introduction to his edition of his philosophical treatises, an account colored by Porphyry's own concerns. After completing his studies in Alexandria Plotinus attempted, by joining a military expedition of the Roman emperor Gordian III, to make contact with the

Brahmins in order to learn something of Indian thought. Unfortunately Gordian was defeated and killed (244). Plotinus somehow managed to extract himself and we next hear of him in Rome where he was able to set up a school of philosophy in the house of a high-ranking Roman lady by the name of Gemina. It is, perhaps, surprising that he had no formal contacts with the Platonic Academy in Athens, which was headed at the time by Longinus, but Longinus was familiar with his work, partly at least through Porphyry who had studied in Athens. The fact that it was Rome where Plotinus set up his school may be due to the originality of his philosophical activity and to his patrons. He clearly had some influential contacts, not least with the philhellenic emperor Gallienus (253–268), who may also have encouraged his later failed attempt to set up a civic community based on Platonic principles in a ruined city in Campania.

Plotinus' school was, like most ancient schools of philosophy, relatively small in scale, but did attract distinguished students from abroad and from the Roman upper classes. It included not only philosophers but also politicians and members of the medical profession who wished to lead the philosophical life. His most famous student was Porphyry (233–305) who, as a relative latecomer to the school, persuaded him to put into writing the results of his seminars. It is almost certain that we possess most, if not all, of his written output, which represents his mature thought, since he didn't commence writing until the age of forty-eight. The school seemingly had inner and outer circles, and Plotinus himself was clearly an inspiring and sympathetic teacher who took a deep interest in the philosophical and spiritual progress of his students. Porphyry tells us that when he was suffering from severe depression Plotinus straight away visited him in his lodgings to help him. His concern for others is also illustrated by the fact that he was entrusted with the personal education of many orphans and the care of their property and careers. The reconciliation of this worldly involvement with the encouragement to lead a life of contemplation is encapsulated in Porphyry's comment that "he was present to himself and others at the same time."

The *Enneads* of Plotinus is the edition of his treatises arranged by his pupil Porphyry who tried to put shape to the collection he had inherited by organizing it into six sets of nine treatises (hence the name *"Enneads")* that led the reader through the levels of Plotinus' universe, from the physical world to Soul, Intellect and, finally, to the highest principle, the One. Although Plotinus undoubtedly had a clearly structured metaphysical system by the time he began committing himself to expressing his thought in written form, the treatises themselves are not systematic expositions, but rather explorations of particular themes and issues raised in interpreting Plato and other philosophical texts read in the School. In fact, to achieve his neat arrangement Porphyry was sometimes driven even to dividing certain treatises (e.g., III.2–3; IV.3–5, and VI.4–5).

Although Plotinus' writings are not transcripts of his seminars, but are directed to the reader, they do, nevertheless, convey the sort of lively debate that he encouraged in his school. Frequently he takes for granted that a particular set of ideas is already familiar as having been treated in an earlier seminar that may or may not be found in the written text. For this reason it is useful for the reader to have some idea of the main philosophical principles of his system as they can be extracted from the *Enneads* as a whole.

Plotinus regarded himself as a faithful interpreter of Plato whose thought lies at the core of his entire project. But Plato's thought, whilst definitive, does according to Plotinus require careful exposition and clarification, often in the light of other thinkers such as Aristotle and the Stoics. It is because of this creative application of different traditions of ancient thought to the interpretation of Plato that Plotinus' version of Platonism became, partly through the medium of later Platonists such as Porphyry, Iamblichus (245–325), and Proclus (412–485), an influential source and way of reading both Plato and Aristotle in the Middle Ages, the Renaissance, and up to the early 19th century, when scholars first began to differentiate Plato and "Neoplatonism." His thought, too, provided early Christian theologians of the Latin and particularly of the Byzantine tradition, with a rich variety of metaphysical concepts with which to explore and express difficult doctrinal ideas. His fashioning of Plato's ideas into a consistent metaphysical structure, though no longer accepted as a uniquely valid way of approaching Plato, was influential in promoting the notion of metaphysical systems in early modern philosophy. More recently increasing interest has centered on his exploration of the self, levels of consciousness, and his expansion of discourse beyond the levels of normal ontology to the examination of what lies both above and beneath being. His thought continues to challenge us when confronted with the issue of humanity's nature and role in the universe and of the extent and limitations of human knowledge.

Whilst much of Plotinus' metaphysical structure is recognizably an interpretation of Plato it is an interpretation that is not always immediately obvious just because it is filtered through several centuries of developing Platonic thought, itself already overlaid with important concepts drawn from other schools. It is, nevertheless, useful as a starting point to see how Plotinus attempts to bring coherence to what he believed to be a comprehensive worldview expressed in the Platonic dialogues. The Platonic Forms are central. They become for him an intelligible universe that is the source and model of the physical universe. But aware of Aristotle's criticism of the Platonic Forms as lifeless causes he takes on board Aristotle's concept of god as a self-thinker to enable him to identify this intelligible universe as a divine Intellect that thinks itself as the Forms or Intelligibles. The doctrine of the Forms as the thoughts of god had already entered Platonism, but not as the rigorously argued identity that Plotinus proposed. Moreover the Intelligibles, since they are identical with Intellect, are themselves actively intellectual; they are intellects. Thus Plato's world of Forms has become a complex and dynamic intelligible universe in which unity and plurality, stability, and activity are reconciled.

Now although the divine Intellect is one it also embraces plurality, both because its thoughts, the Intelligibles, are many and because it may itself be analyzed into thinker and thought. Its unity demands a further principle, which is the cause of its unity. This principle, which is the cause of all unity and being but does not possess unity or being in itself, he calls the One, an interpretation of the Idea of the Good in Plato's *Republic* that is "beyond being" and that may be seen as the simple (hence "one") source of all reality. We thus have the first two of what subsequently became known as the three Hypostases, the One, Intellect, and Soul, the last of which acts as an intermediary between the intelligible and physical universes. This last Hypostasis takes on all the functions of transmitting form and life that may be found in Plato, although Plato himself does not always make such a clear distinction between soul and intellect. Thus the One is the ultimate source of all, including this universe, which is then prefigured in Intellect and transmitted through Soul to become manifest as our physical universe. Matter, which receives imperfectly this expression, is conceived not as an independently existing counter-principle, a dangerously dualist notion, but is in a sense itself a product of the One, a kind of non-being that, while being nothing specific in itself, nevertheless is not simply not there.

But this procession from an ultimate principle is balanced by a return movement at each level of reality that fully constitutes itself only when it turns back in contemplation of its producer. And so the whole of reality is a dynamic movement of procession and return, except for matter, which has no life of its own to make this return; it is inert. This movement of return, which may be traced back to the force of "love" in Plato or Aristotle's final cause, is characterized by Plotinus as a cognitive activity, a form of contemplation, weaker at each successive level, from Intellect through discursive reasoning to the merest image of rational order as expressed in the objects of the physical universe.

The human individual mirrors this structure to which we are all related at each level. For each of us has a body and soul, an intellect, and even something within us that relates to the One. While it is the nature of soul to give life to body, the higher aspect of our soul also has aspirations toward intellect, the true self, and even beyond. This urge to return corresponds to the cosmic movement of return. But the tension between soul's natural duty to body and its origins in the intelligible can be, for the individual, a source of fracture and alienation in which the soul becomes over-involved and overwhelmed by the body and so estranged from its true self. Plotinus encourages us to make the return or ascent, but at the same time attempts to resolve the conflict of duties by reconciling the two-fold nature of soul as life-giving and contemplative.

This is the general framework within which important traditional philosophical issues are encountered, discussed and resolved, but always in a spirit of inquiry and ongoing debate. Issues are frequently encountered in several different contexts, each angle providing a different insight. The nature of the soul and its relationship to the body is examined at length (IV) using the Aristotelian distinctions of levels of soul (vegetative, growth, sensitive, rational) whilst maintaining the immortal nature of the transcendent soul in Platonic terms. The active nature of the soul in sense-perception is maintained to preserve the principle that incorporeals cannot be affected by corporeal reality. A vigorous discussion (VI.4 and 5) on the general nature of the relationship of incorporeals to body explores in every detail and in great depth the way in which incorporeals act on body. A universe that is the product of design is reconciled with the freedom of the individual. And, not least, the time-bound nature of the physical universe and human reason is grounded in the life of Intellect, which subsists in eternity. Sometimes, however, Plotinus seems to break outside the framework of traditional metaphysics: the nature of matter and the One, each as non-being, though in a different sense, strains the terminology and structure of traditional ontology; and the attempt to reconcile the role of the individual soul within the traditional Platonic distinction of transcendent and immanent reality leads to a novel exploration of the nature of the self, the "I."

It is this restless urge for exploration and inquiry that lends to the treatises of Plotinus their philosophical vitality. Whilst presenting us with a rich and complexly coherent system, he constantly engages us in philosophical inquiry. In this way each treatise presents us with new ideas and fresh challenges. And, for Plotinus, every philosophical engagement is not just a mental exercise but also contributes to the rediscovery of the self and our reintegration with the source of all being, the Platonic aim of "becoming like god."

While Plotinus, like Plato, always wishes to engage his audience to reflect for themselves, his treatises are not easy reading, partly no doubt because his own audience was already familiar with many of his basic ideas and, more importantly, had been exposed in his seminars to critical readings of philosophical texts that have not survived to our day. Another problem is that the treatises do not lay out his thought in a systematic way but take up specific issues, although always the whole system may be discerned in the background. Sometimes, too, the exact flow of thought is difficult to follow because of an often condensed mode of expression.

Because we are convinced that Plotinus has something to say to us today, we have launched this series of translations and commentaries as a means of opening up the text to readers with an interest in grappling with the philosophical issues revealed by an encounter with Plotinus' own words and arguments. Each volume will contain a new translation, careful summaries of the arguments and structure of the treatise, and a philosophical commentary that will aim to throw light on the philosophical meaning and import of the text.

John M. Dillon
Andrew Smith

Acknowledgments

I AM GRATEFUL TO John Dillon and Andrew Smith for commissioning this volume for their series and for their comments on my draft typescript. I should also like to thank the late Suzanne Stern-Gillet for sharing her article in *Ancient Philosophy* 39 (2019) with me while it was still in proof as well as Gale Carr, Eliza Tutellier and the editorial team at Parmenides Publishing for all their work on the production of the book.

Abbreviations

Armstrong Armstrong, A. H. 1966–82. *Plotinus*. Greek Text with English Translation and Introductions. Cambridge (MA): Loeb.

DK Diels-Kranz. *Die Fragmente der Vorsokratiker*. 6th ed. Berlin: Weidmann, 1961.

HS_1 Henry, P. and Schwyzer, H.-R. 1951–73. *Plotini Opera* I-III (editio maior). Paris: Desclée de Brouwer et Cie.

HS_2 Henry, P. and Schwyzer, H.-R. 1964–82. *Plotini Opera* I-III (editio minor, with revised text). Oxford: Clarendon Press.

HS_3 Henry, P. and Schwyzer, H.-R. 1973. *Addenda et Corrigenda ad textum et apparatum lectionum*. In HS_1, t. III.

HS_4 Henry, P. and Schwyzer, H.-R. 1982. *Addenda et Corrigenda ad textum et apparatum lectionum*. In HS_2, t. III.

HS5	Schwyzer, H.-R. 1987. "Corrigenda ad Plotini Textum." *Museum Helveticum* 44, 181–210.
SVF	Von Arnim, H., ed. 1905–1924. Stoicorum Veterum Fragmenta. Leipzig: Teubner.

Introduction to the Treatise

THIS TREATISE, I.8 [51], is one of the latest in the chronological order of the *Enneads*, the fifty-first out of a total of fifty-four. Porphyry in his *Life of Plotinus* (6, 16–25) reports that it was one of a final group of four treatises received from Plotinus not long before his death in 270 CE, the others being II.3 [52] *On Whether the Stars are Causes*, I.1 [53] *What is the Living Thing? What is Man?* and I.7 [54] *On the Primal Goods and the Other Goods.* The group of five treatises sent in the preceding year included I.4 [46] *On Well-Being*, the two treatises on providence, III.2 [47] and III.3 [48], and the treatise on love, III.5 [50]. The topics of these treatises suggest that in the last years of his life Plotinus was particularly concerned with ethical issues. I.8 should be understood in this context: its primary purpose is to argue that evil is not intrinsic to the soul. However, since Plotinus always considers ethical issues within a metaphysical framework, the treatise includes an account of the metaphysical status of matter and a nuanced presentation of the way in which matter and the soul can together be responsible for moral evil.

By the time he sent I.8 to Porphyry, Plotinus was no longer teaching. Nevertheless the structure of the treatise reflects a teaching context: it begins by posing the questions to be discussed in Chapter 1 and presents the essentials of Plotinus' answer to those questions in Chapters 2–5; that answer is then supported by interpretation of Plato in Chapters 6 and 7, while Chapters 8–15 address possible objections. Plotinus may well have been drawing on earlier teaching of this material.[1] For example, the complex argument of Chapter 6, that there can be a contrary to the Good, is presented in a way which allows us, if we read it carefully, to share the experience of Plotinus' students: it begins by saying that "We must examine" what is meant by Plato's words in *Theaetetus* 176a–177a, before moving away from textual exegesis to a series of questions and answers that use the notion of contrariety found in Aristotle's *Categories* to develop a Plotinian definition of contrariety; according to that definition, the claim made in the *Theaetetus,* that there is something contrary to the Good, becomes quite acceptable. If we find this chapter hard to follow, it is because we do not fully share either the intellectual background of Plotinus' students or their expectations that discussion of philosophical questions

1 Cf. O'Meara (1999, 13–15).

should be grounded in the textual tradition that was so important to them.

In I.8 Plotinus stresses that matter is evil while, paradoxically, insisting that it is ultimately derived from the Good. The extent to which Plotinus offers a consistent account of the generation of matter is the subject of scholarly debate. In the Commentary I argue that I.8.14, 49–54 is consistent with the view expressed in III.4.1, III.9.3, 7–14 and elsewhere that matter is generated by the soul.[2] Plotinus never presents matter as an independent principle or subscribes to any form of metaphysical dualism. At the same time, the firm denial in I.8 that evil is inherent in the soul may seem inconsistent with passages from earlier treatises such as III.9 [13] 3, 7–16 and V.1 [10] 1, 1–6 which can be read as implying that evil originates in the soul. In order to understand the complexity of Plotinus' position on these issues, it is necessary to know something of the philosophical and religious background. The next section of this Introduction will therefore describe some of the key elements in that background, with the aim of showing how Plotinus is responding to ideas found in Plato, Aristotle, the Stoics and Middle Platonists such as Numenius as well as the challenge presented by Gnosticism. Once that background has been set out, I shall explain how it is possible to understand Plotinus' views in a way which

2 See Commentary 14, 49–54 and the scholarly literature cited there.

does preserve the overall consistency of his account of evil, matter, and the soul.

Two centuries after Plotinus, Proclus (412–485 CE) subjected Plotinus' theory of evil to serious criticism. Consideration of that criticism brings into relief the distinctive features of Plotinus' treatment. This Introduction will therefore conclude with a brief account of the objections brought by Proclus against the arguments of I.8 in his monograph *On the Existence of Evils.*

The philosophical background

Plato

I.8, like all of Plotinus' work, is shot through with reminiscences of Plato. Plotinus at one and the same time appeals to Plato as an authority, uses arguments drawn from the dialogues, and offers his own interpretations of individual passages. The details of his use of Plato in this treatise can be found in the Commentary. Here I shall focus on some key texts which are of particular importance for I.8, as well as mentioning one notable omission.

In the *Timaeus* Plato puts into the mouth of Timaeus a story about the formation of the world by a divine craftsman, the demiurge. Timaeus stresses the goodness of the world which is produced, taking the Platonic Forms as a model (28b–29b). At the same time he describes that world as "a mixture of intellect and necessity" in which rational order is imposed on a somewhat mysterious receptacle (47e–49a), later described as the space in which the four elements of water, air, fire and earth combine to form regular solids which are the basis of all physical things (52a–56c). This mythical account, introduced in 29c–d as a "likely story," posed many problems for subsequent interpreters. Plotinus held that the "likely story" was not to be taken literally and that the world had no beginning in time. Like Plato, he believed that order, rationality, and goodness go together and, just as Plato in the *Timaeus* has recourse to vague and mythical language about "necessity" and a "receptacle" to explain the aspects of the world that are disordered, irrational, and lacking in goodness, so Plotinus in I.8.7 invokes *Timaeus* 47e–49a as authority for regarding matter as evil. Evil is similarly presented as an inevitable aspect of human life in *Theaetetus* 176a–177a, a passage which Plotinus expounds at length in I.8.6 and 7. On the one hand he takes this passage as authority for his belief that intelligible reality is completely free from evil while on the other he uses Socrates' argument that there must always be something contrary to the good to support his own understanding of how evil exists as the contrary of good.

A different approach to the presence of evil in the world can be found in Plato's *Laws* where in X 896a–897d the Athenian Stranger suggests that there might be two kinds of soul controlling the world, one good and one evil.

Some Middle Platonist interpreters such as Plutarch used this suggestion in interpreting the *Timaeus* and argued that the evil in the world was due to an evil world soul.[3] Plotinus will have none of this and there are no references to this passage of Plato in 1.8.[4] There are, however, a good many references to Plato's *Phaedo* which make clear that Plotinus' view of the human soul is the same as that found in the *Phaedo*: he believes that the soul's true home is in the intelligible world and that it becomes evil only when it enters into matter.

As a Platonist, Plotinus thinks of reality and value as fundamentally linked. In Plato's *Republic* the Forms are described as "what is" (see, e.g., *Republic* V 480a) while the Good is said to be "beyond being" (see *Republic* VI 509b). In I.8.2 Plotinus offers an outline of the three hypostases of his metaphysical system, the Good (which elsewhere he often calls "the One" or "the First"), Intellect and Soul, and at the beginning of I.8.3 he says firmly, "If then these are the things that are and this is that which is beyond those things, evil would not be situated among the things that are, nor in what lies beyond them, for these are good." It follows that, in looking to Plato, his supreme textual

3 See Plutarch, *On the Generation of the Soul in the Timaeus* 1014E–1015B.

4 Plotinus does use this passage of *Laws* X elsewhere but quite selectively, emphasizing the beneficent powers and activities of soul and making no mention of the possibility of a second, evil kind of soul: see III.1.8.8; IV.7.8[1], 7–8; IV.7.8[4], 12; V.1.2, 1–5, 29–30.

authority, for a way of answering his questions about the nature and source of evils, Plotinus turns first not to any of the Platonic texts on evil mentioned above but to the discussion in the *Sophist* of "what is not" (see *Sophist* 255e–259b and Commentary 3, 3–6 and 6–9). His strategy is to determine the metaphysical status of evil, along lines suggested by the *Sophist*, as "something different from what is," before identifying that something with matter as he conceives it and then addressing the question of the source of evil in the soul. It is only when he has given an account of the place of evil within his overall Platonist metaphysics that he turns to supporting that by exegesis of passages of Plato more obviously concerned with the problem of evil.

Aristotle

A number of Aristotelian ideas appear in I.8, although Aristotle is not mentioned by name. In accordance with his overall approach to Aristotle,[5] Plotinus takes over some key concepts from Aristotelian metaphysics but develops them in directions of his own. In Chapter 3 he employs Aristotle's distinction between accidental and essential characteristics and uses the word *ousia* in the Aristotelian sense of "substance," but at the end of the chapter he transforms Aristotle's notion of matter as that which underlies contraries into something of his own

5 On Plotinus' attitude to Aristotle, cf Karamanolis (2006, Ch. 6).

(see Commentary 3, 16–18, 21–24, 35–40). In Chapter 6 he makes use of Aristotle's argument in *Categories* 5.3b24–4b19 that substances do not have contraries, but argues for his own notion of contrariety which allows him to accept the view that there is something contrary to the Good (see Commentary 6, 17–21, 27–30, 31–38, 39–47). In Chapter 8, responding to an objection claiming that ignorance and wicked desires are due to the combination of matter and form in the body, he appeals to Aristotle's example of the axe in *On the Soul* 2.1.412b12 and *Parts of Animals* 1.642a10–11 (see Commentary 8, 10–13). In Chapter 10 he defines quality in Aristotelian terms and uses Aristotelian language in describing matter as a "substrate" and quality as "accidental" (see Commentary 10, 1–6 and 6–11). Finally, Chapter 11 addresses an objection that uses the Aristotelian concept of privation, countering it with arguments and language taken from Plato (see Commentary 11, 1–6 and 10–19).

Stoicism

The Stoics were committed to a belief in divine providence and were prepared to explain many phenomena that strike us as evil as having an ultimately good purpose: Chrysippus thought that bed-bugs are useful for waking us and that mice encourage us not to be untidy; less entertainingly, he was even prepared to argue that the Trojan War was devised by the gods as a means of population control (see

Plutarch, *On Stoic Self-contradictions* 1044D and 1049B). Plotinus' two treatises on providence, III.2 and III.3, show some influence of Stoic views of this kind.[6] The Stoic God is a rational, active principle, immanent in the world. Matter is the passive principle on which God acts; in itself it has no qualities and so is neither good nor bad (see Diogenes Laertius 7.134 and Alexander of Aphrodisias, *On Mixture* 224.32–225.3). Plotinus has a very different view, both of God and of matter: he shares the Stoics' monism but completely rejects their materialism, holding that the divine source of good, order and rationality in the physical world lies in a higher, transcendent realm and in I.8.10 he argues against the Stoic view that matter has no qualities and, as such, cannot be evil.[7] In I.8 Plotinus is more concerned with evil in the human soul than with the cosmic perspective adopted in III.2 and III.3. In I.8.14 he argues against the view that vice is "a weakness in the soul," a view which he expresses in terms that reflect elements of Stoic psychology and epistemology (see Commentary 14, 1–7). He makes clear that for him the soul has descended into the body from the intelligible world and that evil in the soul is not to be explained in Stoic terms but as a

6 See Sharples (1994) for more details.

7 On the relationship between Plotinus' view of matter and that of the Stoics, especially in II.4, see Long (2016, 41–44) and Long (2022, 18–27).

complex interaction between matter, as he understands it, and the individual soul.

Middle Platonism

The issues addressed in I.8 were much discussed by the Platonists before the time of Plotinus; we are accustomed to calling these philosophers "Middle Platonists" as a way of distinguishing their thought from that of Plotinus and his successors.[8] Of these, two are particularly important for the understanding of I.8. The work *On the Generation of the Soul in the Timaeus* by Plutarch (c. 45–120/5 CE) takes the form of an extended commentary on *Timaeus* 35a–36b on the formation of the world soul. It appeals to precisely the passage of *Laws* X, 896a–897d, ignored by Plotinus and argues that there are two world souls, one good and one bad, the bad one being responsible for evil in the world and in individual souls. Plotinus' predecessor, Numenius of Apamea, who was active during the second century CE, did not subscribe to this view but, according to Calcidius' Latin commentary on the *Timaeus* written in the fourth century CE, held that evil was due to matter, which he regarded as an independent principle (see Numenius

8 Dillon (1996) offers a broad survey of Middle Platonist thought. Boys-Stones (2018) provides an accessible collection of texts in translation, with commentary. For discussion of which thinkers count as "Middle Platonists" and why, see Boys-Stones (2018, 1–23).

fragment 52 des Places[9]). Plotinus is firmly opposed to the kind of view found in Plutarch but also wishes to avoid the dualism implied by the view of Numenius. In I.8 we can see him steering a path between these two positions.

Gnosticism

Gnosticism was a religious movement, or group of movements, popular in the Roman Empire in the first and second centuries CE. Much of our evidence for Gnosticism comes from their critics rather than from Gnostic writers themselves, although the discovery of a collection of Coptic Gnostic texts at Nag Hammadi in 1945 has opened up new possibilities for understanding the Gnostics on their own terms. Some Gnostics, such as Basilides or Valentinus, were attacked by their fellow-Christians as heretics. Others were regarded by pagan philosophers as deviant Platonists. In Chapter 16 of his *Life of Plotinus* Porphyry lists a whole series of authors, some of whose names are also attached to texts in the Nag Hammadi collection. Porphyry says that Plotinus produced refutations of these thinkers in his seminars and in the work to which he (Porphyry) gave the title *Against the Gnostics,* that is II.9 [33]. II.9 is the fourth and final part of a long treatise, all directed against Gnosticism, which Porphyry split up

9 For a detailed account of Middle Platonist theories of matter and evil, including translations of relevant texts, see Boys-Stones (2018, 103–124).

into sections to conform to his thematic arrangement of the *Enneads*, the other three parts being III.8, V.8, and V.5.

The key feature of Gnosticism to which Plotinus took exception is the belief that the world in which we live is the product of an error by a lesser divine being and is therefore essentially evil. Within this world are trapped some divine sparks, elect souls which can be awakened to an understanding (*gnōsis*) of their true nature and so return to the higher world from which they came. In Chapter 23 of the *Life* Porphyry offers an alternative title for II.9, "Against those who say that the Universe and its Maker are Evil," which makes very clear how Plotinus' view differs from that of the Gnostics: he does not regard either the maker of the universe (the demiurge of the *Timaeus*) or the universe itself as evil. In the anti-Gnostic treatises Plotinus argues against the Gnostic account of the production of the world, setting out instead his own view that the world is generated by a kind of contemplation (see III.8.1–7) and attacking the Gnostics as arrogant thinkers who offer perverse interpretations of Plato, tell false stories about how the universe came into being and make false claims to control higher powers by magic and to cure diseases by casting out evil spirits, wrongly despising the beauty that can be found in the material world which is an image of the intelligible and can remind us of it (see II.9.6, 9–14, 16–18).

Some scholars have thought that Plotinus' controversy with the Gnostics led to an evolution in his view of the generation of matter, and of evil, and that in I.8 his position on these topics is different from that found in earlier treatises.[10] In the next section of this Introduction I shall argue that this is not the case—but even if it were, it is clear that Plotinus never accepts any version of Gnosticism, any more than he accepts the views of Numenius and Plutarch outlined above. Having seen both what Plotinus owes to his predecessors and also something of the way in which his views differ from theirs, I turn now to the interpretation of I.8 itself.

Evil, matter, and the soul in I.8

There has been considerable scholarly discussion over the interpretation of I.8. Dispute has focused on the question of how far this treatise is consistent with the views about evil, matter, and the soul found in earlier treatises of Plotinus. The interpretation which I shall present here is essentially that which Denis O'Brien has argued for and defended in numerous publications from 1971 onwards.[11] As we have seen, Plotinus wishes to avoid the kind of dualism espoused by Numenius as well as to distance himself

10 See especially Narbonne (2001, 113–147) and, in more detail, Narbonne (2006) and (2007).

11 See in particular O'Brien (1971), (1993), (1996).

from the views of the Gnostics. Although he regards matter as evil, he does not believe that it is an independent principle, of equal status with the Good. He uses Plato's *Sophist* in Chapter 3 and Aristotle's *Categories* in Chapter 6 to argue that evil has a peculiar metaphysical status: it "is not" in the sense that it is "other than what is" and exists as a contrary to the Good. This allows Plotinus to recognize the existence of evil in the world (and indeed to regard such existence as inevitable, as Socrates does in Plato's *Theaetetus*), but at the same time to insist that the Good is primary and that even evil depends upon it.

In identifying evil with matter, Plotinus is identifying it with the lowest level in a world ultimately derived from the Good. Each level in Plotinus' metaphysical system is generated by the level prior to it. Thus the Good (the One) generates Intellect and Intellect generates Soul (see V.1.6–7, V.2.1, V.4.2). The One and Intellect generate by a kind of "overflowing" which is also described, somewhat paradoxically, in terms of a lower hypostasis turning back towards a higher one and contemplating it. So, for example, in V.2.1, 7–18 Plotinus writes: "The One, perfect because it seeks nothing, has nothing and needs nothing, overflows, as it were . . . and its superabundance makes something other than itself. This, when it has come into being, turns back upon the One and is filled, and becomes Intellect by looking towards it . . . Resembling the One thus, Intellect produces in the same way . . . This activity springing from the substance of Intellect is Soul, which comes to be while Intellect abides unchanged." Soul too generates, but not in quite the same way, as Plotinus goes on to explain in V.2.1, 18–21: "But Soul does not abide unchanged when it produces . . . It looks to its source and is filled, and going forth to another opposed movement generates its own image." This image is nature, the power which animates the physical world in a way which is described in III.8 as a kind of contemplation; as we have seen, this forms part of Plotinus' argument against the Gnostic view of the world as evil.[12] In III.4.1 Plotinus describes how nature, as the lowest level of soul, also generates. Its product, matter, is described as "lifeless," "shapeless," and "absolutely indefinite." In III.9.3, 7–16 the generation of matter is ascribed to "the partial soul" which "wishing to be directed towards itself . . . makes an image of itself, the non-existent, as if walking on emptiness and becoming more indefinite."

These passages present matter in very passive terms; similarly, in II.4.5, 18 matter is described as merely "a decorated corpse." A few passages in I.8 appear to describe matter in more active terms. This has led some interpreters to argue that I.8 is closer to dualism than earlier treatises.[13] However, it is clear from I.8.2 and 3 that Plotinus' overall

12 For a brief account of what Plotinus means by "nature," with references to further passages of the *Enneads*, see O'Meara (1993, 77).

13 See especially Schwyzer (1973).

view of the place of matter and evil in his system remains the same as before.[14] He uses the vivid imagery of passages such as 4, 20–25, 8, 13–24 and 14, 35–36 at points where he is particularly concerned to argue that evil is not intrinsic to the soul and that without the existence of matter, there would be no evil. Such imagery should not be taken at face value (see Commentary 4, 17–22; 8, 13–24; 14, 25–37).

Matter, then, for Plotinus, is evil in the sense that it is a necessary cause of the inevitable existence of evil in the world, but it does not produce evil on its own. Rather, in his view, evil arises from the interaction of matter with the individual soul. In some passages in earlier treatises Plotinus writes as though souls are responsible for cutting themselves off from the intelligible world. We have seen above that the account of the generation of matter in III.9 [13].3, 7–16 describes the partial soul as "wishing to be directed towards itself." Similarly, V.1 [10].1, 1–6 declares that "the beginning of evil for them [souls] was audacity . . . and the wishing to belong to themselves." However he offers what looks like a rather different view in another early treatise, IV.8 [6], where moral evil is treated as a product of the soul's association with the body rather than as the cause of that association. In IV.8.5, 24–33

14 See also Commentary 7, 16–23 and cf. II.4.16, 16–25; III.2.5, 26–29; III.6.11, 27–45 with the comments in Fleet (1995, 206–208); V.9.10, 18–20.

he describes the soul as descending "by a spontaneous inclination" but says that "if it escapes quickly it takes no harm," while in the previous chapter, at 4, 13–30, he explains how "being in the fetters of the body" prevents the soul from "acting by intellect." The view for which Plotinus argues in I.8 is similar to that presented in IV.8. The language used in III.9.3, 7–16 and V.1.1, 1–6 reflects the context of those passages: in III.9 he is more concerned with the generation of matter by the partial soul than with how evil arises, while in V.1 he starts from the situation of the fallen soul, which is like a child estranged from its parents. The use of the word "audacity" (*tolmā*) there does suggest that the soul's descent is voluntary—but a related verbal form, *tolmēsas* ("daring"), also appears in I.8.9, 18. For Plotinus, the voluntary and the necessary do not exclude one another. In IV.8.5 he attempts to explain how souls voluntarily accept what is necessarily laid upon them, ascribing the descent of souls to a god in line 13 but referring, as we have seen, to "a spontaneous (*autexousios*) inclination" in line 26.[15]

In I.8 Plotinus' position is most fully expounded towards the end of the treatise, in Chapter 14, but is also implied in earlier chapters. Souls descend from the intelligible realm and enter into bodies. Here they are in the presence of matter, the necessary cause of evil. Some souls become "infected" by contact with matter, to use

15 See also Commentary 9, 18–19 and Atkinson (1983, 4–6).

Plotinus' own metaphor in 4, 22 and 8, 16, and thus turn to evil. The fact that these souls are open to such infection, although not the cause of their becoming evil, is nevertheless a sufficient condition for it: they would not become evil if they were not liable to infection but if they are so liable, becoming evil is bound to follow once they are in the presence of matter. The evil in such souls is thus due both to matter and to their own state. Nevertheless, just as not everyone who comes in contact with an infectious disease falls ill, so not all souls turn to evil and the soul is not intrinsically evil; it is always possible for a soul to turn in the other direction, back towards its intelligible source, as Plotinus stresses in 15, 23–28.

Plotinus' position is thus complex, but consistent both within I.8 and throughout his work. He avoids both the Scylla of the view found in Plutarch, that there is an evil world soul, and the Charybdis of the view found in both Numenius and the Gnostics, that matter is an independent, evil principle. He does his best to preserve a belief in the dependence of all things on a single, supremely good First Principle while admitting that there is evil in the world. He offers a subtle account of the origin of evil in the soul as caused not by either the soul or matter on its own but by the combination of the two. However, his position is open to criticism on two, related grounds. First of all, one might ask whether Plotinus' ingenious account of how matter can be evil and yet ultimately generated by the Good is really coherent. Secondly, he can be criticized for failing to offer an adequate explanation, either in I.8 or elsewhere, for the descent of the soul into body. It has been pointed out that for Plotinus, as for Aristotle and the Stoics, action can be voluntary without being chosen and that he is quite happy to describe the descent of the soul as both voluntary and necessary.[16] While this makes it possible for Plotinus to reconcile the different approaches to the descent of the soul found in different Platonic dialogues, it does not solve the problem of how far souls which allow themselves to become "infected" by matter are responsible for what happens to them. In III.2.4, 36–44 he says that "living beings which have of themselves a movement under their own control (*autexousios*) might incline sometimes to what is better, sometimes to what is worse" and describes how "a deviation which is slight to begin with" may produce "a settled choice (*hairesis*)."[17] This passage suggests a similar account to that offered in I.8 of how a soul may become evil but, like I.8, still leaves it unclear how far the soul is responsible for inclining one way or another. Both the coherence of Plotinus' account of matter and the adequacy of his treatment of the descent of

16 See IV.8.1, 29–48, IV.8.5, 1–4 and IV.3.13, 14–20 with the discussion by O'Brien (1977).

17 Cf. III.3.4, 47–48 and O'Meara (1993, 85).

the soul were criticized by the later Neoplatonist, Proclus, to whose critique of I.8 I now turn.

Proclus on I.8

While Proclus shares Plotinus' monism and his belief in the overall goodness of the world, his account of the metaphysics of evil is quite different. Proclus regards evil as a *parhypostasis* or "parasitic existence," a phenomenon rather like the harmful side-effects of a beneficent drug, which arises in things below the level of the intelligible because of their material and divided nature. He set out this view and criticized Plotinus' position, sometimes implicitly, sometimes explicitly, in his commentaries on Plato, in a commentary on the *Enneads* which no longer survives and, above all, in his monograph *On the Existence of Evils.*[18] In Chapters 30–37 of *On the Existence of Evils* Proclus summarizes the argument of Plotinus I.8.3 and then criticizes it on the grounds that matter is necessary but not evil; it cannot be evil because it is generated from the divine. Chapter 31 presents the dilemma very clearly: according to the principles of Neoplatonist metaphysics,

18 See Proclus, *Commentary on Plato's* Timaeus I.373.22–383.21, *Commentary on Plato's* Republic I.37.23–39.1. A scholion on the second passage refers to lost commentaries by Proclus on the speech of Diotima in Plato's *Symposium* and on Plato's *Theaetetus* as well as to his commentary on Plotinus and the monograph *On the Existence of Evils*: see Proclus, *Commentary on Plato's* Republic II.371.12–18.

causes are greater than their effects or products, and those effects or products tend to assimilate themselves to their causes. If the One, which is the principle of good, generates matter, then matter must be good to some degree. Alternatively, if matter is itself a principle of evil, there must be two first principles, one of good and the other of evil, a conclusion which Proclus, like Plotinus, firmly rejects. This dilemma implies that the argument for the necessity of evil offered by Plotinus in I.8.7, 16–23 is invalid.[19]

Rather than holding that matter is generated by the partial soul, as Plotinus did, Proclus regards it as simply the lowest level of the unlimited which is generated from God, that is, from the One. He supports his argument by appealing to Plato, *Philebus* 26c4–27c1, where the principles of all things are said to be limit, unlimited, and the cause of the mixture of the two, which Proclus identifies with God.[20] At the end of Chapter 37 he argues, against Plotinus' view in I.8.6, that there is nothing contrary to the Good, maintaining the Aristotelian view of contraries rather than the Plotinian modification of that view.[21] In Chapter 38 he discusses the relationship between matter, evil, and privation and argues that privation of form is not

19 Cf. Commentary 7, 16–23.

20 Cf. *On the Existence of Evils* (2003, 120n242 and 121n250).

21 See also *On the Existence of Evils* 45.15–17 and Commentary 6, 17–21; 27–30; 31–38; 39–47; 54–59.

evil.[22] He goes on to argue, in Chapter 47, that there is no single cause of evils and to explain, in Chapters 49–50, what he means by calling evil a *parhypostasis.*

Whereas Plotinus held that a part of our soul never descends from the intelligible world,[23] Proclus subscribed to the more pessimistic view of Iamblichus, according to which the human soul descends entirely. In his *Commentary on the* Timaeus III.313.19–24 and 333.28–334.9 Proclus emphasizes that the Iamblichean view implies that the soul is responsible for moral evil. We should not then be surprised to find Proclus arguing against Plotinus' view of the origin of evil in the soul. In Chapters 20–26 of *On the Existence of Evils* Proclus addresses the question of evil in souls, arguing in Chapters 23–24 that the weakness of human souls in particular is present in them *before* they come into contact with matter. In Chapter 33 he reiterates this point and presses the problem raised by Plotinus' account: "If . . . souls are drawn by matter—that is, if we attribute the cause of their generation to the attraction matter exercises upon souls, as something that draws them—where is their self-motion and ability to choose?"[24]

These criticisms by Proclus are effective in highlighting difficulties in Plotinus' arguments in I.8, although it may be doubted whether the alternatives which Proclus

22 Cf. Plotinus I.8.11.

23 See Plotinus IV.8.8, 1–6.

24 *On the Existence of Evils* (2003, 82, lines 22–25 Boese).

offers are any more satisfying. Proclus offers some acute criticisms of Plotinus' arguments and puts forward an alternative account of the metaphysics of evil. The disagreement between Plotinus and Proclus can also be seen as a disagreement over the interpretation of Plato's *Timaeus.* Where Plotinus takes *Timaeus* 47e–49a as warrant for regarding matter as evil, Proclus makes clear in *On the Existence of Evils* Chapter 32 that he understands the "receptacle" of the *Timaeus* as something more like Aristotelian matter, a neutral substrate.[25] Although Plotinus and Proclus, as Platonists, share many fundamental assumptions, the differences between their treatments of the metaphysics of evil are instructive in showing how much scope there was within the Platonic tradition for diverse interpretations of Plato's texts and different philosophical positions.

On the issue of evil in the soul, Proclus at first sight appears again to be an effective critic of Plotinus, pressing the problem of the soul's responsibility for wrongdoing. Yet Proclus does not want to follow Plutarch and others in postulating an evil world soul, any more than does Plotinus.[26] The problem of how a providential divine plan can allow for the making of choices by individual souls remains. In *Ten Problems Concerning Providence* V 31

---

25 Cf. Commentary 7, 1–7.

26 See Proclus, *Commentary on the* Timaeus I.382.2–11 and cf. *On the Existence of Evils* 40.5–8.

Proclus describes how when the rational soul descends into a human body an irrational soul also comes to exist in such a way that the rational soul lives in a manner contrary to its nature, while in *On the Existence of Evils* Chapter 24 he talks of "weakness" in the soul causing its descent. He notes that "all things do not have the same mode of weakness" and appeals to Plato, *Republic* X 617d and *Phaedrus* 248c to justify the claim that some souls become associated with mortality and "fall to earth." These passages of the *Republic* and the *Phaedrus* form part of Plato's mythical accounts of how souls choose their lives. Insisting that the soul chooses the life it lives while in the body does offer a way of attributing responsibility for evil to the soul rather than to matter. However, an appeal to "weakness" as the reason why some souls choose morally inferior lives does not solve the problem of reconciling divine providence with moral responsibility; it simply describes that problem in a different way. Whereas Plotinus would say that someone who lives a wicked life has a soul which has become evil as a result of its contact with matter, Proclus would say that such a person has a "weak" soul which chose the wrong kind of life when it descended into the body. Just as Plotinus in I.8.15, 23–28 stresses that it is always possible for a soul to turn back towards its intelligible source, so Proclus in *On the Existence of Evils* Chapter 24 turns from the *Republic* and the *Phaedrus* to the *Timaeus*, citing 42c–d on the possibility of return from successive reincarnations. As with their differences over the metaphysics of evil, the differences between Plotinus and Proclus are in part differences over the interpretation of Platonic texts dealing with the descent of the soul.

Conclusion

I began this Introduction by stating that the primary purpose of I.8 is to argue that evil is not intrinsic to the soul. Comparison of Plotinus' views with those of Proclus brings out clearly how and why they disagree over the nature and source of evils. They both share Plato's conviction that the soul has descended from, and can return to, a higher, intelligible world, but Plotinus' belief that a part of our soul never descends leads him to emphasize that evil arises in the soul as a result of its interaction with matter. His account of matter as generated by the partial soul and yet a necessary cause of the existence of evils in the world is vulnerable to criticisms such as those of Proclus; nevertheless it remains an ingenious attempt to defend monism and the essential goodness of the soul while recognizing the existence of evils. Throughout the treatise, Plotinus writes as a teacher and an interpreter of Plato, seeking to justify his views by appealing to the authority of Platonic texts. He asks questions of his readers, challenges their assumptions, and makes them think.

While it may be necessary to refer to the Commentary to understand the details of Plotinus' argumentation, I hope anyone who has begun reading this volume by reading the Introduction will now turn immediately to the Translation and engage for themselves with his discussion of the topic.

Note on the Greek Text

Line numbers in the translation are approximate and do not always match the original Greek text. Since the commentary follows the sequence of the English translation, there may sometimes be a slight discrepancy in the ordering.

The Greek text adopted is that of the Oxford edition, that is, the *editio minor* (for comparison between readings in HS_1 and HS_2 see vol. 3, xiii–xiv). Deviations from the text are noted in the commentary. Passages of Plotinus from treatises other than I.8 in the Introduction and the Commentary are taken from Armstrong 1996–1982 and 1989, occasionally with modifications.

Each *Ennead* is referred to by Roman numerals, followed by the number of the treatise, the chapter of the treatise, and, finally, separated by a comma, the line number or numbers, for example, VI.8.8, 24–27, that is, *Ennead* VI, treatise number 8, Chapter 8, lines 24–27.

It is customary to add the chronological number given

by Porphyry in his *Life of Plotinus* (*Vita Plotini*), so that, for example, VI.8 is designated VI.8 [39], that is, *Ennead* VI.8 is 39th in the chronological order. So we adopt the convention as follows: either VI.8.8, 1–5 (where the chronological number is not given) or VI.8 [39] 8, 1–5 (where it is given).

In this series the chronological number is given only in the Introduction and in other places where it may be of significance for understanding the chronological presentation of Plotinus' philosophical stance. The following chart indicates the chronological order.

Chronological Order of the *Enneads*

Enn.		*Enn.*		*Enn.*		*Enn.*		*Enn.*		*Enn.*	
I.1	**53**	II.1	**40**	III.1	**3**	IV.1	**21**	V.1	**10**	VI.1	**42**
I.2	**19**	II.2	**14**	III.2	**47**	IV.2	**4**	V.2	**11**	VI.2	**43**
I.3	**20**	II.3	**52**	III.3	**48**	IV.3	**27**	V.3	**49**	VI.3	**44**
I.4	**46**	II.4	**12**	III.4	**15**	IV.4	**28**	V.4	**7**	VI.4	**22**
I.5	**36**	II.5	**25**	III.5	**50**	IV.5	**29**	V.5	**32**	VI.5	**23**
I.6	**1**	II.6	**17**	III.6	**26**	IV.6	**41**	V.6	**24**	VI.6	**34**
I.7	**54**	II.7	**37**	III.7	**45**	IV.7	**2**	V.7	**18**	VI.7	**38**
I.8	**51**	II.8	**35**	III.8	**30**	IV.8	**6**	V.8	**31**	VI.8	**39**
I.9	**16**	II.9	**33**	III.9	**13**	IV.9	**8**	V.9	**5**	VI.9	**9**

	Enn.		*Enn.*		*Enn.*		*Enn.*		*Enn.*		*Enn.*
1	I.6	**10**	V.1	**19**	I.2	**28**	IV.4	**37**	II.7	**46**	I.4
2	IV.7	**11**	V.2	**20**	I.3	**29**	IV.5	**38**	VI.7	**47**	III.2
3	III.1	**12**	II.4	**21**	IV.1	**30**	III.8	**39**	VI.8	**48**	III.3
4	IV.2	**13**	III.9	**22**	VI.4	**31**	V.8	**40**	II.1	**49**	V.3
5	V.9	**14**	II.2	**23**	VI.5	**32**	V.5	**41**	IV.6	**50**	III.5
6	IV.8	**15**	III.4	**24**	V.6	**33**	II.9	**42**	VI.1	**51**	I.8
7	V.4	**16**	I.9	**25**	II.5	**34**	VI.6	**43**	VI.2	**52**	II.3
8	IV.9	**17**	II.6	**26**	III.6	**35**	II.8	**44**	VI.3	**53**	I.1
9	VI.9	**18**	V.7	**27**	IV.3	**36**	I.5	**45**	III.7	**54**	I.7

Synopsis

Chapter 1

1–6 The questions to be discussed: the nature of evil, where it comes from and what kind of existence it has.

7–20 How is it possible for us to understand evil? How can evil be contrary to good?

Chapter 2

1–9 The Good is the principle of all things and self-sufficient. It is not itself beautiful but is beyond beauty.

9–25 The hypostasis of Intellect is not like the discursive reasoning that human beings use. It is a unity-in-multiplicity whose contents are the Platonic Forms. It comes from the Good and reverts to it. Likewise, the hypostasis of Soul constantly looks upwards, to Intellect and the Good.

25–32 There is no evil in the first two hypostases or in Soul when it is looking up towards them. This is supported by what Plato says in *Phaedrus* 248 and *Letter* 2.312.

Chapter 3

1–12 Evil belongs with what is not, that is to say, with something different from what is. The sensible world, along with the involuntary affections and false opinions associated with that world, belongs with what is not; so does the principle which underlies all these.

12–20 That which is essentially evil lacks all the characteristics of the Good.

21–40 That which is essentially evil lacks measure, limit, and form. Evils of body and soul are secondary to this primary evil, which is to be identified with underlying matter. Such matter is no more than an image of what is.

Chapter 4

1–6 The evil in bodies, secondary evil, is due to matter which is primary evil. Unlike matter, soul is not evil in itself; not all soul is evil.

6–12 What is the evil soul? It is the soul whose irrational part is liable to lack of measure, to excess and deficiency and so to vices and false opinions.

12–22 What causes this evil in the soul? The irrational part of the soul becomes evil only when the soul has descended into a body. The rational part of the soul too, when it has descended into the body, can become damaged and "infected" by matter which makes like itself that which comes into contact with it.

25–32 The rational, perfect soul which remains pure and turned towards Intellect contrasts with the soul which turns away towards matter. Such a soul is deficient and indeterminate; it "sees darkness."

Chapter 5

1–5 An objection: defining evil as "lack of good" implies that there is a principle of evil beyond matter.

5–19 The objection is rejected. There are degrees of lack or deficiency. Only matter does not participate in the Good at all and so is utterly deficient. Matter does not even have being. Total lack—as in matter—involves evil while "great lack" occurs in the individual soul that can fall into evil. Evil in itself, generic evil, should be distinguished from specific evils in the soul such as particular vices.

19–26 What about poverty and disease? Disease, ugliness, and poverty can all be explained as due to matter.

26–34 The origin of evil does not lie in the human soul. Some human beings can free themselves from evil and there is no evil in the "perceptible gods," the heavenly bodies, even though they are material.

Chapter 6

1–9 What does Plato mean when he claims that evils are a necessary feature of life on earth? Does he mean that there is no evil in the heavens because of their regular movement?

9–17 The words "escape from this place" in *Theaetetus* 176a refer to escaping from vice. According to Plato, evils exist of necessity because there must be something contrary to the good.

17–27 Vice is contrary not to the Good but to human moral virtue. How can anything be contrary to the Good? Is it always the case that if one of a pair of contraries exists, the other also exists? Plato is not saying that, but he does say that there is a contrary to the Good.

27–38 It has been proved (by Aristotle) that particular substances do not have contraries, but this has not been proved for substance in general. What would be contrary to universal substance and to the first principles (including the Good, which is beyond substance)? The contrary of substance is non-substance; the contrary of good, as a whole, is evil, as a whole.

39–47 Contraries are "the furthest apart from each other." Good and evil have contrary characteristics. Just as falsehood is contrary to truth, so the being of the evil nature is contrary to the being of the divine, good nature.

47–54 If fire and water were distinct substances, they would be contraries in themselves but in fact both fire and water are constituted by matter, which takes on the contrary qualities of hot and dry, wet and cold to form fire and water respectively.

54–59 Contrariety does not depend on quality or on any particular category of being but on things being separated from each other as much as possible.

Chapter 7

1–7 The All, that is, the physical universe, necessarily contains matter and contraries, as Plato confirms in the *Timaeus* and the *Politicus*.

7–16 *Theaetetus* 176a–177a on the necessity of evil is supported by the words which the demiurge addresses to the younger gods in *Timaeus* 41b. In Plato's view the way to escape from the mortal realm is to acquire virtue, separating oneself from the body, and from matter.

16–23 Procession from the Good, the highest principle, must come to an end at a final point, matter, which is evil because good is completely absent from it.

Chapter 8

1–10 Objection 1a: ignorance and wicked desires are due not to matter but to the combination of matter and form in the body.

10–28 Two answers to Objection 1a:

(i) Forms in matter require matter in order to be effective.

(ii) Matter corrupts and infects enmattered forms. This is like the way in which the characteristics of an animal's food are changed in the process of digestion.

So the objection implies that matter is responsible for evil.

28–29 Objection 1b (a reply to the answers given to 1a): matter should be mastered by the soul.

29–37 The answer to Objection 1b: our desires and judgements are affected by our bodily state.

37–44 Vice is secondary evil, not evil itself.

Chapter 9

1–5 How do we know evils? How do we know vice?

5–14 The only way in which we can know absolute vice is by abstraction. We know partial vice by its lack of virtue, just as we identify ugliness in a face, for example, by its lack of form.

14 How can we know matter which is completely formless?

15–26 We can know matter in two ways:

(i) by abstraction

(ii) by an experience which is like leaving light in order to see darkness.

Chapter 10

1 Objection 2: how can matter be evil if it is without quality?

2–16 The answer to Objection 2: matter does not have qualities, but it has a nature which is evil in a non-qualitative sense.

Chapter 11

1–9 Objection 3: if evil consists in privation, it will always be in something else, and evil in the soul will not be due to anything external. Whether there is no such thing as matter or matter exists but is not evil, the origin of evil lies in the soul.

10–19 The answer to Objection 3: the soul is, of its nature, both alive and good; it follows that the soul cannot be primary evil, nor can such evil be an accident of it.

Chapter 12

1–3 Another version of Objection 3: evil in the soul consists in partial, rather than complete, privation of good.

3–7 The answer to this version of Objection 3: any such evil would not be primary evil as it would not be unmixed.

Chapter 13

1–2 Objection 4: evil is an impediment which produces evil within the soul.

2–14 The answer to Objection 4: such an impediment would itself be the product of something external to the soul. Vice might be described as an impediment of this kind, but it is only a secondary evil, just as virtue is only a secondary good.

14–26 In extreme cases, the soul may descend so completely into evil that it can no longer be called a soul at all. Such a descent may be described as sinking, as falling into dark mud, and as dying.

Chapter 14

1–8 Objection 5: vice is a weakness in the soul.

9–24 The answer to Objection 5: the soul can be described as weak only by analogy with the body. Only souls that have entered into matter can become evil and unable to perform their function; souls which are not in matter are pure and their function is unimpeded.

25–49 The relationship between matter and soul: soul has no spatial location; matter restricts the expression of the many powers of the soul, begging and causing trouble; matter is illuminated by soul and yet weakens it by its presence.

49–54 Matter is evil before soul is. It is the presence of matter which brings about evil in the soul.

Chapter 15

1 Objection 6: Matter does not exist.

1–3 The answer to Objection 6: the necessity of matter's existence has been shown elsewhere.

3–4 Objection 7: Evil does not exist.

4–9 The answer to objection 7: the existence of evil is implied by the existence of good and by the existence of desire, avoidance, and intellection.

9–23 The world in which we live is one in which good and evil are mixed. Desires (other than the desire for intellect), emotions, imagination, and false opinion are all due to soul's contact with matter.

23–28 The evil in the world is like prisoners bound in chains of gold. It may be hidden and, even when we see it, we also see images of the beautiful which remind us of the intelligible.

Translation of Plotinus Ennead *1.8 [51]*

On the Nature and Source of Evil

1. Those who enquire into the source of evils—whether they enter into reality in general or into a particular kind of reality—would make an appropriate beginning for their enquiry if they first posed the question of what evil is and what is its nature. That is how | understanding would be gained of where evil came from, where it sits and in what it occurs accidentally, and in general there would be agreement as to whether it exists in reality.

There is another problem: by which of the powers in us could we understand the nature of evil, if understanding of each thing comes by likeness? For intellect and soul, since they are Forms, would also | produce understanding of Forms and their desire would be directed towards them; but how could anyone imagine that evil is a Form when it appears in the absence of all good?

But if, given that contraries are objects of the same knowledge and evil is contrary to good, knowledge of good will also be knowledge of evil, | then those who intend to understand evils must have a clear perception of good, since the better precede the worse and are Forms, while the worse are not Forms but rather are privation.

All the same, there is also a question as to how good is contrary to evil: perhaps one is the beginning and the other is the last point, or one is Form and the other is privation— | but this is to be discussed later.

2. Now let us say what is the nature of the good, as far as is appropriate for the present discussion. It is that on which everything depends and "which all beings yearn for;"[27] they have it as their principle and are in need of it. It lacks nothing, is sufficient | to itself, in need of nothing, a measure and a limit for all things, giving from itself intelligence, being, soul, life and intellectual activity. All things are beautiful up to this point, for it itself is beyond beauty, beyond the best, ruling as king in the intelligible world.

Intellect in that world is not what one might think of | by analogy with our so-called intellects which are full of propositions and able to understand what is said: they reason discursively and examine what follows, looking at reality in sequence since they did not have a grasp of it

27 Aristotle, *Nicomachean Ethics*, 1.1.1094a3.

earlier but remained empty until they learned, | despite being intellects. Intellect in that world is not like this, but has all things and is all things; it is with them when it is with itself and has all things without having them. For it is not other than them, nor is each thing in it separate, for each one is the whole and complete in every way, and yet they are not confused but each is separate in a different sense. | At any rate, that which participates in it does not participate in everything at once but participates in what it can. That intellect is the first activity coming from the Good and the first being, while the Good abides in itself; intellect, however, is active around it and, so to speak, lives around it.

Soul dances around intellect on the outside and by gazing at it and | contemplating its interior, views god through it. This is the "carefree," blessed "life of the gods;"[28] evil is nowhere here and if things had stopped there, there would not have been any evil but only the first and the second and third order of goods: "all things are around the king of all, and that is the cause | for all things, and all things belong to that and the second around the second things and the third around the third."[29]

3. If then these are the things that are and this is that which is beyond those things, evil would not be situated

28 Plato, *Phaedrus* 248c4, a1.

29 Plato, *Letter* 2.312e1–4.

among the things that are, nor in what lies beyond them, for these are good. So it remains that, if evil exists, it is situated among the things that are not; it is, so to speak, a sort of form of what is not | and associated with something that has been mixed with what is not or, in some way or other, participates in what is not. "What is not" does not mean "utter non-being" but only something different from what is. It is not non-being in the same way as the movement and rest which are associated with what is, but as an image of what is or as a still greater degree of non-being. This applies to the whole sensible world and | to all affections associated with the sensible, anything posterior and accidental to these, their principle and any one of the things which make up the whole that is like this.

At this point one might arrive at a conception of evil as a kind of absence of measure in relation to measure, absence of limit in relation to limit, absence of form in relation to that which produces form, always lacking | compared to that which is self-sufficient, always undefined, in no way stable, subject to every sort of affection, insatiable, utter poverty. These characteristics are not accidental to it but are, as it were, its being and whatever part of it you look at is all of these; everything which participates in it and becomes like it becomes evil but is not | essentially evil.

In what sort of entity are these things to be found, not as something different from it but as that entity itself?

If evil is an accident of something else, evil itself must be something prior to this, even if it is not a substance. For just as there is good itself and that which is accidentally good, so too there would be evil itself and that which is accidentally evil, derived from that.

| What then is lack of measure, if it is not in the unmeasured? [And what is measure if not in the measured?]

Well, just as there is measure which is not in the measured, so too there is lack of measure which is not in the unmeasured. For if it is in something else, it is either in something unmeasured—but this something does not need lack of measure since it is itself unmeasured—or in something measured—but it is impossible that | the measured should possess lack of measure according to which it is measured. So too there must be something lacking limit in itself and itself lacking form and the other attributes mentioned earlier which characterize the nature of evil; if there is anything like this posterior to it, either it has evil mixed in with it, or it is like this because it looks towards evil, or because it produces something like this. | So that which underlies figures, forms, shapes, measures and limits, adorned with an order that is alien to it, possessing no good of its own, an image in comparison with the things that are and indeed the substance of evil, if there can actually be a substance of evil—this is what the argument discovers to be primary evil, | evil in itself.

4. The nature of bodies, insofar as it partakes of matter, will be evil, but not primary evil, for bodies have a sort of form which is not true form and are deprived of life: they destroy one another; their movement is disorderly; they impede the soul in its own activity; they escape | being and are always in flux; they are secondary evil. Soul on the other hand is not evil in itself, nor is all soul evil. But what is the evil soul?

It is what Plato is referring to when he says "they have subjected the part of the soul in which evil naturally arises;"[30] that is to say, the irrational part of the soul receives evil, lack of measure, excess, and deficiency, from which | come intemperance, cowardice and all other vice in the soul, involuntary affections that produce false opinions, making the soul believe that the things which it avoids are evil and those which it pursues are good.

But what is it that produces this vice and how are you going to refer it back to the principle and cause of evil that has just been described?

First of all, this kind of soul is not outside matter or on its own. | It follows that it is mixed with lack of measure and has no share in form, which brings order and leads to measure, since it is combined with a body that possesses matter. Next, its reasoning part, if it too is damaged, is prevented from seeing by its passions, by being darkened by matter, by its inclination towards

30 Plato, *Phaedrus* 256b2–3.

matter and in general by looking not towards | being but towards becoming; the principle of becoming is the nature of matter which is so evil that it infects with its own evil that which is not yet in it but only looks towards it. For since it is completely without a share in good and is a privation of it and unmixed deficiency, it makes like itself everything which comes into contact with it | in any way.

The perfect soul which inclines towards Intellect is always pure and turns away from matter; it neither sees nor approaches anything undefined, unmeasured and evil and so it remains pure, completely defined by Intellect. As for the soul which does not stay like this but proceeds out of itself because it is not perfect or primary but is like | a reflection of that first soul, because it is deficient insofar as it falls short—such a soul is filled with indeterminacy and sees darkness; at that moment it possesses matter by looking at what it does not look at, just as we are also said to "see" darkness.

5. "But if lack of good is the cause of seeing and associating with darkness, evil for the soul would also lie in the lack [or in the darkness] and this would be primary evil—let the darkness be a secondary evil—and the nature of evil would no longer be in matter but even before | matter."

No: evil is not in just any kind of lack but in total lack; at any rate what lacks the good only a little is not evil for it can even be perfect as regards its own nature. But when there is total lack, as there is in the case of matter, this is real evil, with no share in good. | For matter does not even have being, so as to share in this feature of the good, but "is" applies to it homonymously so that it would be true to say that it "is not." So lack involves not being good, total lack involves evil, and great lack involves the possibility of falling into evil and is already evil. Accordingly, evil should be thought of not | as this or that particular evil, such as injustice or any other vice, but as that which is not yet any of these; these are, as it were, species of evil, formed by additions; for example, wickedness in the soul and its species are made specific by the matter concerned or by the parts of the soul or by the fact that one is like a sort of seeing while another is like an impulse or an experience.

But if | someone supposes that things external to the soul, such as disease or poverty, are evil too, how will he refer them to the nature of matter?

Disease is deficiency and excess of material bodies that do not maintain order and measure, ugliness is matter not mastered by form, and poverty is want and privation of things which we need because of | the matter to which we have been joined, a matter whose nature is neediness. If this is rightly said, we should not suppose that we are the origin of evil as being evil in ourselves; evils are prior to us. The evils that take hold of human beings take hold of them against their will; there is an "escape from evils in the soul"[31] for those | who are capable of it, but not everyone is capable. Although matter is present to the perceptible gods, evil, the vice which human beings have, is not, since not even all humans have it; these gods master matter—though the gods in whom matter is not present are better—and they master it by that in them which is not in matter.

6. We must examine what Plato means when he says that evils "cannot be destroyed" but exist "of necessity;" they do not exist "among the gods, but always prowl around mortal nature and this place."[32] Does this mean that the heavens | are "pure of evils"[33] because they always move regularly and proceed in order, with no injustice or other vice there, no wronging of one another, but proceeding in order, while injustice and disorder exist on earth? For this is "mortal nature and this place."

But the words "escape from this place"[34] no longer | refer to life on earth. For "escape," Plato says, is not leaving earth but being "just and pious with wisdom"[35] even

31 Plato, *Phaedo* 107d1.

32 Plato, *Theaetetus* 176a5–8.

33 Plato, *Theaetetus* 177a5.

34 Plato, *Theaetetus* 176a9.

35 Plato, *Theaetetus* 176a9–b2.

while on earth; he means we must escape from vice, and it follows that for him evils are vice and everything that comes from vice. And when the interlocutor says evils would come to an end if "he persuaded | people" of what he is saying, Socrates replies that this "could not happen;" for evils exist of necessity, since "there must be something contrary to the good."[36]

How is it possible for human vice to be the contrary of the Good? For human vice is contrary to virtue, and this is not the Good but | a good which makes mastery of matter possible. How could anything be contrary to that Good? For it has no quality.

Then is it universally necessary that if one of a pair of contraries exists, the other should also exist?

Granted that it is possible and may indeed be the case that when one contrary exists, the other does too—for example, when health exists, disease can also exist—| nevertheless this is not necessarily so. Perhaps Plato does not necessarily mean that this is true of every contrary; he is talking only about the Good.

But if the Good is substance, how can there be anything contrary to it? Or to what is beyond substance?

That there is nothing contrary to substance has been reliably | proved by induction in the case of particular substances; it has not been proved for substance in general.

36 Plato, *Theaetetus* 176a2–7.

But what would be contrary to universal substance and in general to the first principles?

The contrary of substance is non-substance, and whatever is the nature and principle of evil is contrary to the nature of good; for both are originating principles, the one of evils, the other of goods. Everything included in the one nature will be contrary to things included in the other, | so that even the wholes are contraries and more contrary to each other than the rest. For the other contraries belong either to the same species or to the same genus and in consequence have something in common.

As for things which are separate, where one of a pair contains the contraries of those characteristics which contribute to constituting the essential nature of the other member of the pair, | could they not be the most contrary of all if "contraries are the furthest apart from each other?"[37]

Indeed, lack of limit, lack of measure and all the other characteristics which the evil nature has are contrary to limit, measure and all the characteristics which the divine nature contains, so that the whole too is contrary to the whole. And the evil nature has a false being and | is falsehood primarily and in reality; the being of the divine nature is true being, so that, just as falsehood is contrary to truth, the being of the evil nature is contrary to the being of the divine.

37 Aristotle, *Categories* 6.6a17–18.

So we have shown that it is not true in every case that substance has no contrary. Besides, in the case of fire and water too we would have accepted that they were contraries | if they did not have a common element, matter, in which hot and dry and wet and cold occur as accidents. If they existed by themselves, constituting their substance on their own, without what they have in common, there would be contrariety here too, a contrariety of one substance to another. Therefore things which are completely separate, have no common element, | and are by nature as far apart as they can be—those things are contraries; contrariety does not depend on quality or, in general, on any particular category of being, but on things being separated from each other as much as possible, composed of opposing elements and producing contrary effects.

7. How then is it necessary that if the Good exists, evil also exists?

Is it because there must be matter in the All? For this All is necessarily composed of contraries; it would not exist if matter did not. For indeed "the nature of this universe is a mixture of intellect and necessity"[38] | and everything which comes to it from God is good while the evil things

38 Plato, *Timaeus* 47e5–48a1.

come from “the ancient nature,”[39] by which Plato means the underlying matter that has not yet been ordered.

What does he mean by “mortal nature,” given that “this place”[40] refers to the All?

The answer is: “But since you have come into being, | you are not immortal, but thanks to me you will not be dissolved.”[41] If this is the case, it would be correct to say that “evils cannot be destroyed.”[42]

So how is one to escape?

Not by change of place, says Plato, but by acquiring virtue and separating oneself from the body and thus also from matter, since association with the body is also association with matter. | Plato explains somewhere what separation is and what it is not; being “among the gods”[43] means being among the intelligibles, for these are immortal.

The necessity of evil can also be grasped in the following way. Since the Good is not the only thing that exists, there must be a last point to the process of going out from it or, if one prefers to put it like this, to the continual going down and falling away, a last point | after which nothing else could come into being, and this is evil. What follows

39 Cf. Plato, *Politicus* 273b5.

40 Plato, *Theaetetus* 176a7–8.

41 Plato, *Timaeus* 41b2–4.

42 Plato, *Theaetetus* 176a5.

43 Plato, *Theaetetus* 176a7.

the first must necessarily exist and so the last must also exist; this is matter which has nothing at all of the first. That is how evil is necessary.

8. Suppose someone were to say that we do not become evil because of matter, since neither ignorance nor wicked desires are due to matter; even if they come into existence as a result of bodily evil, they are produced not by matter but by form, | for example by heat, cold, bitter, salt and all kinds of humor, as well as by fillings and emptyings—not fillings without qualification, but fillings with such-and-such; in general, that sort of thing is what produces the difference in desires and, if you like, in faulty judgements, so that form rather than matter | is evil.

Even someone who says this will nonetheless be forced to concede that matter is evil. For the quality in matter does not do what it does when it is separate, just as the shape of the axe does not do anything without the iron. Then too the forms in matter are not the same as they would be if they existed on their own; | as material principles they are corrupted in matter and are infected with its nature. Not even fire burns by itself, nor do any other things by themselves produce what they are said to do when they are in matter. For matter takes control of what is manifested in it and corrupts and destroys it, | applying its own contrary nature, not by opposing cold to heat, but by opposing its own formlessness to the form of heat, applying its shapelessness to shape and its excess and deficiency to the measured until it has made the form belong to it, matter, and no longer to itself. Similarly, when animals take in nourishment, | that which has been taken in does not remain as it came, but becomes dog's blood and all that makes a dog, and all the humors become everything which belongs to the animal that receives them. Indeed, if body were responsible for evils, in this way too matter would be responsible for evils.

Someone else might say that matter should be mastered.

But that which could master it is not pure unless it escapes. | Also, desires become stronger as a result of such mixing with bodies and different people's desires vary in strength, so that the individual's power cannot master them. Some people's judgement is dulled because they are chilled and impaired by bodily evil; contrary states make people unstable. Our dispositions | at any given moment are also evidence of this: when we are full, we are different, in both our desires and our thoughts, from when we are empty, and we are different when we are filled in one way from when we are filled in another.

Let the unmeasured then be primary evil and let that which comes to be in unmeasuredness, either by likeness or by participation, be secondary evil, because its lack of measure is accidental. In the same way, darkness is primary and that which is darkened | is secondary.

Now vice, which is ignorance and lack of measure in the soul, is secondary evil and not evil itself, for virtue is not primary good either but is that which has become like it or has participated in it.

9. With what, then, do we know these evils? First, with what do we know vice? For we know virtue by intellect itself and by wisdom, since wisdom knows itself. But how do we know vice? Just as we use a ruler to know what is straight and what is not, so too we know what does not fit with virtue. So do we know it by seeing it | or by not seeing it, vice, I mean?

We do not see absolute vice, for that has no limit. So it is by abstraction that we know that which is in no way virtue and we know partial vice by its lack of virtue. So we see a part and by the part which is there, we grasp what is not there, which is in the complete form but | is not in that part, and so we speak of vice, leaving undefined that which is deprived of form. Likewise when, for example, we see an ugly face in matter, when the rational principle has not taken charge within it so as to hide its ugliness, we picture it to ourselves as ugly because it lacks form.

What about something which has not encountered form at all?

| Completely abstracting all form, we call matter that in which there is no form; we ourselves actually grasp shapelessness in the abstraction of all form, if we are going

to look at matter. For this reason this is actually another intellect, which is not intellect, daring to see what does not belong to it. It is like when an eye turns away from the light | in order to see darkness and not see it—it leaves the light in order to see the darkness since it cannot see it with the light, but without this it cannot see but can only not see—it turns away so as to see insofar as that is possible. In this way intellect too, leaving its own light inside itself and, as it were, going forth outside itself, going to what does not belong to it, | without bringing its own light, experiences the contrary of what it is so that it may see its own contrary.

10. That is how this is. But if matter is without quality, how can it be evil?

Matter is said to be "without quality" in the sense that it does not have in itself any of the qualities which it will receive and which will be in it as a substrate, but not in the sense that it has no nature.

| Well, if it has some nature, what prevents this nature from being evil, but not evil in a qualitative sense?

Quality is that in virtue of which something else is said to be qualified. So quality is accidental and in something else, whereas matter is not in something else, but is the substrate to which the accidental relates. | It is said to be "without quality" because it does not possess the quality which has the nature of an accident.

Moreover, if quality itself is without quality, how could matter, which has not received quality, be said to possess quality? Therefore matter is rightly said to be both without quality and evil, for it is not said to be evil because it has quality, but rather because it does not have it, | so that perhaps it would not have been evil if it were form instead of a nature contrary to form.

11. But the nature which is contrary to all form is privation; privation is always in something else and has no existence in its own right. So if evil is in privation, evil will be in that which is deprived of form, and there will be no evil in itself. In that case, if | there is evil in the soul, the privation in it will be evil and vice, not anything external.

There are some arguments which claim to remove matter entirely, while others say that, though matter exists, it is not itself evil. In that case there is no need to look elsewhere for evil; we should place it in the soul, and so posit it as an absence of good.

| But if the privation is of a form which ought to be present, if it is privation of good in the soul and it produces vice in it by the operation of its own principle, then the soul has nothing good in it, not even life, despite being a soul. Therefore the soul will be soulless, if it does not even have life in it, so that, despite being a soul, it will not be a soul. | It has life by its own principle, and so it does not have privation of the good in its own nature.

It follows that it is of a good kind and has some good in its own nature, a trace of intellect, good and not evil; it is not then primary evil, nor is primary evil an accident of it, because the good is not completely absent from it.

12. But how should we respond if someone says that vice and evil in the soul are not complete privation of good but a partial privation of good?

In this case, if the soul has some good but is also deprived of some, it will have a mixed disposition and the evil will not be unmixed; | the primary, unmixed evil has not yet been discovered. Also, the soul will have the good in its substance but evil as some sort of accident.

13. Then perhaps the soul has evil as an impediment, like something impeding the eye in seeing.

But in that case evil, in their view, is something which produces evil and produces it in such a way that evil itself is something different. So if vice is an impediment to the soul, it will be something which produces | evil, but not the evil; and virtue is not the good except insofar as it co-operates with it; and so if virtue is not the good, vice is not the evil. Then too, virtue is not the beautiful itself or the good itself; so it follows that vice is not the ugly itself nor the evil itself. We did say that virtue is not | the beautiful itself nor the good itself because the beautiful itself and the good itself are prior to it and transcend it;

it is good and beautiful by some kind of participation. Then just as, ascending from virtue, we reach the beautiful and the good, so too, descending from vice, we reach the evil itself, taking vice as the starting-point. We will contemplate it | with the contemplation which belongs to evil itself and will participate in it as we become it; for we come to be entirely in "the place of unlikeness,"[44] when sinking into it we have fallen into dark mud. If too the soul falls completely into complete vice, it no longer has vice but has exchanged its nature | for a worse one, for vice mixed with something of its contrary is still human. So it dies, insofar as a soul can die, and its death, while it is still plunged in the body, is sinking in matter and being filled with it and, when it has left the body, lying there until it stirs again and somehow lifts its gaze from the | mud—this is "going to Hades and falling asleep there."[45]

14. But suppose someone says that vice is a weakness in the soul—that the evil soul is prone to passion and easily moved, carried along from one evil to another, easily moved to desires, easily provoked to fits of anger, precipitate in assents | and yielding readily to faint impressions, like the weakest products of art or nature which are readily destroyed by breaths of wind and the heat of

44 Plato, *Politicus* 273d6–e1.

45 Plato, *Republic* VII 534c7–d1.

the sun—then it will be worth enquiring into the nature and source of this weakness in the soul.

Well, weakness in the soul is not like weakness in bodies. | In bodies lack of ability to perform their function and being easily affected are called weakness; the word "weakness" would apply to the soul by analogy—unless the cause of its weakness were the same, namely matter. But we must address the question of the cause for what is called weakness in the soul more directly; for it is not | density or rarity or thinness or fatness or a disease, like a fever, which makes the soul weak. This kind of weakness of soul must occur either in souls which are completely separate or in those which are enmattered or in both. If it does not occur in souls which are separate from matter—for they are all pure | and, as Plato says, "winged and perfect"[46] and their function is unimpeded—it remains that the weakness must be in fallen souls which are not pure and have not been purified; their weakness will not be a removal of anything, but the presence of something alien, like phlegm or bile in the body.

| When we grasp the cause of the soul's fall more clearly and as it should be grasped, then what we are looking for, the weakness of soul, will be obvious. There is matter in reality and there is soul and there is, so to speak, one place for both of them. For there is not one place for matter and another, separate place for soul—for

46 Plato *Phaedrus* 246b7–c1.

example, matter in earth | and soul in air—but the soul's separate place is not being in matter, that is, not being united with matter. This means that no unit comes into being from soul and matter, and soul is not in matter as a substrate—this is what being separate is. There are many powers of soul and soul has a beginning, | a middle and an end; matter is there and begs and, so to speak, is importunate and wants to come right inside; but "the whole place is holy"[47] and there is nothing which is without a share in soul. So matter subjects itself and is illuminated. On the one hand, it cannot grasp the source of its illumination—for that source cannot tolerate it, | although it is there, since it does not see matter on account of its being evil. On the other hand, matter darkens the illumination, the light from that source, by mixing itself in with it; it weakens it by itself offering it generation and the cause of coming into matter, for the light would not have come to what was not present.

This is the fall of the soul, coming into matter in this way | and growing weak, because all its powers do not come into action; matter hinders their presence by itself taking over the place which the soul occupies and making the soul "contract,"[48] as it were, and by making evil what it has taken by a kind of theft, until the soul is able to stir again. So matter is the cause of both weakness | and

47 Sophocles, *Oedipus at Colonus* 54.

48 Plato, *Symposium* 206d6.

vice in the soul. Therefore it is itself evil before soul is so, and it is primary evil; for even if the soul itself generated matter in being affected and if it consorted with it, and became evil, matter by its presence is the cause, for soul would not have come to be in it unless its presence had given soul the opportunity for generation.

15. If anyone says that matter does not exist, he must be shown the necessity of its existence from our discussions of matter, where the subject is treated at greater length.

And if anyone says that there is no evil at all in reality, he must | also remove the good and say that there is nothing desirable either, and then that there is neither desire nor avoidance nor intellection; for desire is for good and avoidance is of evil and intellection and wisdom are concerned with good and evil, wisdom itself being one of the things that are good.

So there must be good, unmixed good, | and also that which is a mixture of evil and good; then the mixture, when it has a greater share of evil, makes its contribution to the totality of evil and when it has a lesser share of evil, insofar as it is lessened, it contributes to the good.

Then what would evil be for the soul?

What soul would have it, after all, if it did not have contact with the inferior nature? There would be no desires or | sorrows or passions or fears, for fears belong to the composite which is afraid that it may be dissolved, and sorrows and pains belong to it when it is being dissolved; desires arise when something troubles the composite structure, or when one plans a remedy so as not to be troubled. Imagination comes from a stroke of something affecting the irrational part from outside; it receives the stroke because it is not partless. The soul has false opinions | because it is outside the truth itself; it comes to be outside by not being pure. Desire for intellect is something else; for it needs only to consort with intellect and be established in it, not inclining to the worse.

Owing to the power and nature of good, evil is not only evil; since it appeared of necessity, it is bound | in a sort of beautiful fetters, as some prisoners are chained in gold, and is hidden by them so that, though present, matter may not be seen by the gods, and human beings may have the opportunity not always to look at evil but, even when they do look at it, may consort with images of the beautiful as a reminder.

Commentary

Chapter 1

In this first chapter Plotinus poses the questions to be discussed. The opening sentence raises the two questions mentioned in Porphyry's title for the treatise, but in reverse order: while the title is "On the Nature and Source of Evils," Plotinus, like Plato's Socrates, emphasizes that before one can say anything about X (in this case before one can specify the source of evils), it is necessary to say what X (evil) is. Socrates insists on this point several times in the Meno *(see 71a, 86d–e, 100b) and again in* Protagoras *360e and* Republic *I 354c (cf. also* Laches *189e–190a). This Socratic approach implies that it is possible to identify a single nature and source of evils, and that is indeed what Plotinus will seek in this treatise; the later Neoplatonist, Proclus, took a different approach, both in his monograph,* On the Existence of Evils, *and in his commentary on the* Republic, *1.37.23–39.1 (cf. Introduction, 34–39).*

The perennial question of the source of evils in the world was much discussed during the first three centuries CE by pagan Platonist philosophers as well as by both Christians and Gnostics. Some, such as Plutarch in On the Generation of the Soul in the Timaeus *(6.1014D–1015E), argued that evils were due to a maleficent world soul while others, such as Numenius, saw matter as the source of evils (see Numenius, fragment 52 des Places). Both Plutarch and Numenius were concerned to counter the Stoic view, that God, the active principle, is good and that matter, the passive principle, has no qualities and so is neither good nor bad. Plotinus will deny that soul can be evil; his answer is closer to that of Numenius, but depends on his own, distinctive understanding of matter.*

The question about the source of evils is also expressed as the question whether evils "enter into reality in general or into a particular kind of reality," giving a further indication of what is to come, namely discussion of the status of evil within Plotinus' metaphysics. The second sentence of the chapter articulates these metaphysical concerns in a different way by asking "whether evil exists in reality." The reader does not yet know just how Plotinus will answer the questions posed but it is clear that the discussion will take place within a metaphysical framework. Plotinus then adds two further questions: How is it possible for us to understand evil? And how can evil be contrary to good? The chapter is to some extent programmatic, but Plotinus does not follow the precise order of the questions which it asks; he sets out his view of the nature of evil in Chapter 3 and addresses how we can understand evil in Chapter 9, while the sense in which good is contrary to evil is discussed in the latter part of Chapter 6.

1, 1–2 Plato insists in *Republic* II 379b–c, X 617e and *Laws* X 900e that the gods are not responsible for evil and he excludes evil from the divine realm in *Theaetetus* 176a–177a, a text which Plotinus will expound in Chapter 6. The same view can be found in Aristotle, *Metaphysics* 9.9.1051a19–21. Plotinus himself will argue in Chapter 2 that evil has no place in the intelligible world. The question for him, then, is whether evils "enter into a particular kind of reality" and if so, what kind.

1, 6 *whether it exists in reality*: Plotinus here leaves open the possibility that evil does have some kind of existence, a possibility denied by the Stoics before him and by Proclus after him. At the end of the treatise, in 15, 3–9, he will respond explicitly, though briefly, to those who say "that there is no evil at all in reality."

1, 8 *understanding of each thing comes by likeness*: This idea has a long heritage in Greek philosophy. In *On the Soul (De Anima)* 1.2.404b11–18 Aristotle first cites Empedocles fragment DK B109 and then refers to Plato's *Timaeus* for the belief that the soul is composed of the elements and that it is able to know and perceive these because like is known by like (cf. *Timaeus* 35a–b, 45b–c; see also Aristotle, *On the Soul* 1.2.405b15–19 and *Metaphysics* 2.4.1000b5–6). Later in *On the Soul*, in 3.8.431b26–432a3, Aristotle applies the principle that like is known by like to his own account of perception and thinking, claiming that intellect and sense-perception can receive the forms of their objects because they are themselves forms.

1, 12–13 *contraries are objects of the same knowledge*: This principle is found in Plato, *Phaedo* 97d4–5 (cf. also *Republic* VII 524a) and in Aristotle, *Prior Analytics* 1.1.24a21 and *On the Soul* 3.3.427b5–6 and 3.6.430b22–23. Plotinus makes use of it in I.6.5, 22–25 where he argues that beauty can be understood by examining ugliness.

1, 17–20 Plotinus develops these brief remarks later, in 6, 28–59, where he explains how he understands the idea that good is contrary to evil.

Chapter 2

Before he embarks on answering the questions he has just posed, Plotinus offers an overview of his metaphysical system, starting with an account of the Good in accordance with his statement in Chapter 1 that "those who intend to understand evils must have a clear perception of good." Plotinus often calls the highest level in his system "the One" or "the First" but in this context it is clearly appropriate to call it "the Good." (On the different names Plotinus uses for the highest level in his system, especially in relation to VI.9, see Meijer [1992, 58–64]). He summarizes his view of the Good, Intellect, and their relationship to each other and offers one sentence about the hypostasis of Soul. He stresses that there is no evil at the higher levels in his system, the implication being that evil can appear only when Soul turns away from the contemplation of higher realities; this is the position he will argue for later in the treatise. Towards the end of the chapter he appeals to Platonic authority for his views, quoting from the myth of the Phaedrus *and from a favourite passage of* Letter 2. *In some other texts, such as I.6 and V.1, Plotinus offers accounts of his metaphysical system which start from the situation of the individual soul and move upwards through the hypostases. Here he starts at the top and moves downwards.*

2, 2–3 *It is that . . . beings yearn for"*: Aristotle in *Metaphysics* 12.7.1072b3 describes the Unmoved Mover as producing movement by being loved and in 1072b13–14 describes it as that on which the heavens and the world of nature depend. He describes the good as "that which all things yearn for" in the opening lines of the *Nicomachean Ethics*, 1.1.1094a3 (note that Plotinus turns Aristotle's *panta,* "all things," into *panta ta onta,* "all beings"). For Plotinus these formal characteristics of the good apply to the first of his three hypostases, as he also makes clear in I.7.1, 21–24. Just as there his reference to Aristotle follows immediately after a reference to Plato's description of the Form of the Good, in *Republic* VI 509b8, as "beyond being," so here he moves swiftly to speaking of the Good in a way which makes clear his distinctive understanding of it as the supreme principle.

2, 4–7 Elsewhere, for example in V.5.6, 11–17, Plotinus is reluctant to offer any description of his highest principle. Here, however, bearing in mind what is "appropriate for the present discussion" (2, 1–2), he is more explicit and characterizes the Good in ways that accord with the philosophical tradition within which he is working: self-sufficiency is another of the formal characteristics of the good in Aristotle's *Nicomachean Ethics* (see 1.7.1097b7–8, 14–15; cf. also Plato,

Philebus 60c), while in Plato, *Philebus* 64d and 66a, measure is associated with the highest good and in Plato, *Laws* IV 716c4–5, God is described as the "measure of all things." (For the connection between "measure" and "limit," cf. also *Philebus* 25b.) For Plotinus, the Good is not itself measure and limit but is the source of these in other things; that is why he carefully describes it as "a measure and a limit *for all things*" (cf. VI.8.18, 3 and V.5.4, 13–14). The last part of the sentence lists the first items which emanate from the Good: being, life, and intelligence all belong to Intellect; soul is included in the list by virtue of its "intellectual activity." (On the triad of being, life, and intelligence and its sources see Hadot [1960].)

2, 7–9 Plotinus consistently locates beauty, *to kalon*, in the intelligible world; the Good rules over that world but lies beyond it: cf. I.6.9, 40–42, V.8, VI.7.33, 19–22 and VI.9.4. The words "up to this point," taken by many translators as meaning "up to the Good," may simply mean "up to the level of the entities just described." The description of the Good as "ruling as king in the intelligible world" echoes the language used by Plato of the Form of the Good in *Republic* VI 509d2 and also looks ahead to Plotinus' use of the "three kings" of *Letter* 2.312e1–4 at the end of the chapter.

2, 9–15 Plotinus begins his explanation of the nature of the hypostasis of Intellect by contrasting it with the kind of intellect we human beings have. The key contrast, which Plotinus develops at greater length in passages such as V.3.2–9 and V.8.4–8, is between human discursive reasoning that moves from premises to conclusions, and a comprehensive intuitive understanding in which everything is grasped as a totality. As discursive reasoners we "remain empty until we learn," whereas Intellect knows eternally.

2, 15–21 Now Plotinus turns to describing the hypostasis of Intellect. Intellect is a unity-in-multiplicity whose contents are the Platonic Forms: these are the separate things in Intellect referred to here, in which lower items participate to the best of their ability. On the relationship between Intellect and the Forms, cf. V.9.8, 4–7.

2, 21–23 Here Plotinus attempts to describe the relationship between Intellect and the Good. In V.3.5, 36 and VI.7.40, 18–19 he describes Intellect as "the first activity," an activity which is also described as "life" in VI.9.9, 17 (cf., with Hadot [1960, 112], Aristotle, *Metaphysics* 12.7.1072b26–27). The Good, by contrast, simply "abides in itself;" in I.7.1, 23–24 Plotinus compares the first principle, which abides while everything else reverts to it, with the centre of a circle from which come all the radii.

2, 23–28 Next Plotinus describes Soul in its relationship to Intellect and the Good, looking upwards. The language of dancing and gazing is used more extensively in VI.9.8, 34–45 where the point is the slightly different one that, as individual souls, we are like dancers who sometimes go wrong by turning away and failing to look at the chorus leader (see Meijer [1992, 239–241], Clark [2016, 118–119] and Sheppard [2020, 100–104]). By contrast, the hypostasis of Soul is described here as a dancer who never turns their gaze away. Both here and in VI.9 Plotinus associates the dancing of souls/Soul with the mythical description in Plato's *Phaedrus* of the gods above the heavens who are followed in their "divine dance" (247a7) by souls that have not yet descended. The words "carefree" and "life of the gods" in lines 25–26 are taken from *Phaedrus* 248c4 and a1 respectively.

2, 28–32 The appeal to the authority of Plato in the immediately preceding lines is reinforced by quotation of *Letter* 2.312e1–4. *Letter* 2, although now usually regarded as Neopythagorean in origin, was accepted by the Neoplatonists as a genuine Platonic text. The account of the "three kings" in 312e1–4 is frequently presented by Plotinus as prefiguring his three hypostases. According to Plotinus' interpretation, the One (the Good) is "the king of all," the second, Intellect, is around the Forms ("the second things"), and Soul is around individual souls ("the third things"). My translation of the quotation follows O'Brien (1992, 322n33); cf. also III.9.7, 3, V.1.8, 1–4 and VI.7.42, 14–24. (For further discussion of Plotinus' use of the "three kings" passage see Dörrie [1970] and Saffrey-Westerink [1974].)

Chapter 3

Plotinus now returns to the question "What is evil?" In Chapter 2 he had offered an outline of his metaphysics which makes clear that reality and value go together and that the three hypostases, the One, Intellect, and Soul, are all good. This leads at the beginning of this chapter to the conclusion that evil is "not among the things that are" and belongs with "what is not." Plotinus thus connects the problem of evil with a very old problem in Greek philosophy, the problem of how one can say or think of what is not (cf. Parmenides, DK B52). Plato, in his discussion of this problem in the Sophist, *had suggested that "A is not B" means "A is different from B." Plotinus uses the language of that Platonic discussion to define evil as something which "is not" in this sense, something which is different from the Good and lacks all the characteristics ascribed to the first principle. In the second half of the chapter he makes explicit his view that if there are things that can be described as evil, there must be something which is evil in itself. Despite holding this view, he does not postulate the existence of an independent principle of evil but argues that evil is "that which underlies figures, forms, shapes, measures and limits," that is, matter. Throughout the chapter he alludes to a distinction between things which are only accidentally evil or only participate in evil on the one hand and primary evil on the other; this distinction will be developed further in Chapters 4 and 5.*

3, 1–3 The Greek verb "to be" (*einai*) can also mean "to exist" and "to be real." Plotinus is using participial forms of this verb (*on, onta*) here and in what follows. I have used "is/are" in my translation to reflect the increasing closeness of Plotinus' words to those used in Plato's *Sophist.*

3, 3–6 Plotinus now starts to draw on the discussion of "what is not" in the *Sophist* for an explanation of the metaphysical status of evil. The words "it is, so to speak, a sort of form of what is not" echo *Sophist* 258d6; Plotinus, however, understands the phrase in a way that fits his own context and qualifies the phrase "a form of what is not" with words which make clear his reluctance to call evil a form. In V.8.7, 22–23 Plotinus uses similarly qualified language to describe matter as "a sort of final form." (For more detailed discussion of the relationship between Plotinus' words and the *Sophist* passage, see O'Brien [1996, 174] and [(2012, 62–63].)

3, 6–9 Lines 6–7 echo Plato, *Sophist* 258b3–4 (cf. also 237b7–8 and 258e6–259a1). As in lines 1–6, I have tried in my translation to reflect Plotinus' use of the *Sophist,* following O'Brien (2012, 44–56). Line 8 refers to two of the

Greatest Kinds mentioned in the *Sophist*, Movement and Rest. *Sophist* 254b–255d lists a total of five Greatest Kinds: Movement, Rest, Sameness, Difference, and Being. The Eleatic Stranger, the main speaker in the dialogue, uses these Greatest Kinds in 255e–259b to explain how saying "what is not" is saying "something different from what is." Plotinus moves away from the *Sophist* in suggesting that what is under discussion is "an image of what is" or "a still greater degree of non-being," using language that reflects his hierarchical metaphysics; his point is not just that evil, whatever it is, is different from "the things that are" but that it belongs to a lower level in the overall order of things.

3, 9–12 For Plotinus the sensible world is only an image of higher reality. The words "anything posterior and accidental to these" probably refer to the involuntary affections of the soul and/or the false opinions produced by such affections, mentioned in the next chapter as secondary evils; their principle is primary evil which will turn out by the end of the chapter to be matter, as Plotinus conceives it. "The things which make up the whole that is like this" I take to be the elements (cf. Hager [1977, 445]).

3, 12–16 Plotinus declares that evil lacks the characteristics that had been ascribed to the Good in the two preceding chapters. In 1, 9–20 the Good is implicitly presented as "that which produces form" while in 2, 5 it is explicitly described as "in need of nothing, a measure and a limit for all things." Plotinus describes evil as lacking in all these qualities and to point up the contrast further adds that evil is "always undefined, in no way stable, subject to every sort of affection, insatiable," ascribing to it characteristics similar to those ascribed to the material substrate in the cosmogony of Plato's *Timaeus* 52d6–e4. He brings the list to a climax at the end of the sentence by declaring that evil is "utter poverty," wording which recalls his interpretation elsewhere of the story of Poverty and Plenty in Plato's *Symposium* 203b–c (cf. 14, 35–36, II.4.16, 19–23, III.5.9, 49–53 and III.6.14, 5–26, with the comments in Fleet [1995, 236–239]). The result is something of a paradox: evil is essentially defined by the fact that it lacks everything.

3, 16–18 The distinction between accidental characteristics and those which "are . . . its being (*ousia*)" is Aristotelian although the insertion of the phrase "as it were" (*hoion*) suggests that Plotinus is aware that he is using the distinction in an unAristotelian way.

3, 18–20 Here Plotinus uses Platonist language of participation and likeness, rather than the Aristotelian language of the immediately preceding lines, to express the distinction between secondary and primary evil.

3, 21–24 Plotinus is once again employing Aristotelian language, using the word *ousia* ("being") in the Aristotelian sense of "substance." He continues to assume, as he has done from the beginning of the treatise, that it makes sense to search for a single nature and source of evils, a search that could lead to postulating an independent principle of evil; however, he will avoid developing his argument in the direction of dualism.

3, 25–32 Plotinus develops the previous point with reference to the characteristics which evil has been said to lack in 3, 12–16, that is, the specific characteristics ascribed to the Good in Chapters 1 and 2. The example of measure is treated in some detail, limit and form more briefly. Plotinus' argument that the unmeasured must derive its quality of being unmeasured from a substantive "lack of measure" seems to assume what he is trying to prove.

3, 25–26 *And what is measure if not in the measured?*: These words appear to be an explanatory gloss on what immediately follows and I have accordingly placed them in square brackets, as in the Oxford text.

3, 33–34 These lines again allude to secondary evils. In Plotinus' view the body "has evil mixed in with it" while when the soul errs, it "looks towards evil" and "produces something like this," that is, something evil. Plato in *Timaeus* 47e5 describes the physical world as coming into being as a mixture of necessity and intellect. Plotinus will have more to say about this in 7, 1–7 and will tackle the problem of how the soul can look towards evil and produce evil in Chapters 9 and 13.

3, 35–40 Plotinus concludes that matter is primary evil, understanding matter as a blank substrate with no qualities of its own. Once again he uses Aristotelian language but he transforms Aristotle's notion of matter as that which underlies contraries (see *Physics* 1.7.191a4–23) into something of his own: he brings out the peculiar metaphysical status of matter, and of evil, by describing this underlying matter in Platonist language as an "image" (*eidōlon*) and expressing reluctance to call it "the substance of evil."

Chapter 4

Plotinus begins this chapter with a brief explanation of bodies as secondary evil. He then turns to a preliminary discussion of evil in the soul. As explained in the Introduction, the primary purpose of I.8 is to argue that evil is not intrinsic to the soul. Plotinus will consider the issue more fully in Chapters 11–14. Here he states firmly that evil in the soul is brought about by the soul's contact with matter while in Chapter 14 he will attempt to explain this in more detail.

4, 1–6 Plotinus distinguishes between bodies and matter on the one hand and between bodies and soul on the other. Consistently with the position set out in Chapter 3, he argues that the evil in bodies is due to matter; matter is primary evil while bodies are secondary evil. Before he turns to address the problem of evil in the soul, he reiterates that soul is not evil in itself, unlike matter, and that not all soul is evil, unlike bodies which in his view are all evil, although their evil is secondary, not primary.

4, 3–4 *their movement is . . . its own activity*: This description of bodies recalls *Timaeus* 30a4–5 and *Phaedo* 65a10.

4, 4–5 *they escape being and are always in flux:* Cf. the distinction between the worlds of being and becoming in *Timaeus* 27d7–28a4. For the attribution of fluidity to bodies by earlier Platonists see Pépin (1971, 156n3).

4, 6–12 Plotinus cites Plato, *Phaedrus* 256b2–3 in support of his view that it is the irrational part of the soul which "receives evil." He uses language similar to that used in Chapters 2 and 3 to associate evil with lack of measure, excess and deficiency, regarding these as responsible for vices such as intemperance and cowardice and describing such vices as "involuntary affections" which give rise to false opinions about what to pursue and what to avoid.

While the connection between vices and false opinions goes back to Plato (see, for example, *Meno* 77c–78a, *Gorgias* 467a–468e, 509e5–7, *Laws* IX 860d1–2) this is in some ways a very Aristotelian ethical picture, implying that virtue lies in the mean between excess and deficiency and that the wicked have a mistaken perception of the good: see Aristotle, *Nicomachean Ethics* 2.6–8. However Aristotle holds that the wicked are ultimately responsible for their false opinions about good and evil (see *Nicomachean Ethics* 3.5) whereas Plotinus is reluctant to ascribe responsibility for evil to the soul, preferring to lay the blame on matter; similarly in

III.1.10 Plotinus argues that souls are responsible for their good actions but that when they go wrong external influences are to blame (cf. also I.2.5).

4, 12–17 These lines explain Plotinus' view of the relationship between irrational soul, body and matter, implying that the irrational part of the soul becomes evil only when the soul has descended into a body (cf. II.3.8, 13–15).

4, 17–22 Plotinus turns to how the rational soul, which properly belongs to the intelligible world, can be damaged and "infected" by matter, using the Platonic distinction between "being" (*ousia*) and "becoming" (*genesis*), that is, between the intelligible and sensible worlds. The idea that the soul is damaged by entering into the body goes back to Plato, *Republic* X 611b10–c1 and reappears in other passages of Plotinus such as I.6.5, 32, IV.7.10, 25 and IV.8.5, 28. The talk of the reasoning part of the soul being prevented from "seeing" and "looking towards" the good associates matter with darkness in a way that also has its roots in Plato: the analogies of the Sun, Line and Cave in Plato's *Republic* (VI 506b–VII 518b) depend on a parallel between knowing and seeing; in particular, 515c–517a describe the experience of emerging from the Cave and returning to it as a passage from darkness to light and back again while the language of light and darkness continues to be used in the following passage, 517b–519b, where Socrates tells his interlocutors that the soul needs to be turned around so that it looks in the right direction, upwards rather than downwards. (On Plotinus' use of the language of seeing, light and darkness, including its relationship to Plato's analogy of the Sun, see Beierwaltes [1977, especially 97–107].) The metaphor of infection also comes from Plato, from *Phaedo* 67a4–5; in using it here, Plotinus emphasizes that it is matter which is the cause of evil in the soul and that, before it enters the body, soul is pure and unblemished. (On the way in which such imagery appears to ascribe an active role to matter, cf. Introduction, 29–30 and Commentary 14, 25–37 and 14, 38–43.)

4, 25–32 In the last part of the chapter Plotinus contrasts the rational, perfect soul which remains pure and turned towards Intellect, with the soul which turns away towards matter. He describes such a soul as deficient, indeterminate and "seeing" the darkness of matter, by contrast with the perfect soul which has none of these failings. He is reluctant to use the same language of "seeing" and "looking towards" of the soul which is attracted to matter and so develops the description of matter as "darkness" which we can "see" only in a transferred sense (cf. Commentary 9, 19–26 and II.1.6, 39–41).

Chapter 5

Plotinus begins this chapter by considering an objection, that defining evil as "lack of good" implies that there is a principle of evil beyond matter. He firmly denies this, arguing that matter is utterly deficient ("total lack"), with no share in either good or being. Matter is thus primary evil while both moral and physical evils are secondary. He reiterates that evil in the soul arises, in one way or another, from the soul's association with matter and goes on to explain how physical evils such as disease and poverty are also due to matter. He ends the chapter on a positive note by declaring that some human beings can free themselves from evil and that there is no evil in the "perceptible gods," the heavenly bodies, even though they are material.

5, 1–5 *"But if lack . . . even before matter"*: I have put this sentence in quotation marks in the translation to make clear that it is an objection to what Plotinus has said so far. The "darkness" referred to is matter; I have followed recent editors and translators in placing the words "or in the darkness" in square brackets to indicate that they are a gloss, added to the text by a copyist in an unsuccessful attempt to explain the meaning.

5, 5–9 Plotinus does not wish to compromise his monism by allowing that there is a principle of evil as well as a principle of good; he also wishes to exclude any suggestion that the ultimate source of evil lies in the soul. In response to the objection, he distinguishes between different degrees of lack or deficiency. According to Plotinus' metaphysics, all levels below that of the first principle which is the Good are deficient to some degree but, as he explains, levels such as Intellect and Soul can be "perfect as regards their own nature" (cf. the way in which these levels were described in 2, 15–25); only matter does not participate in the Good at all and so is utterly deficient. The description here of evil as "in total lack" (*elleipsis*) is comparable to the statement in II.4.16, 3 that matter "is the same thing as privation" (*sterēsis*); Plotinus uses the word "privation" later in this chapter, at line 24, and in Chapters 11 and 12 he responds to objections that misunderstand what is meant by the claim that evil is privation.

5, 9 *with no share in good*: These words recall the description of matter as "possessing no good of its own" in 3, 36–37. They also echo several passages of Plato's *Philebus*—20d1, 54c10, 60b3–4—although in the first two of these the phrase "a share in the good" simply refers to the Good; Plotinus' use of it is closest to the third passage (60b3–4), which states that "intelligence has a greater share in the good than pleasure".

5, 9–12 As in 3, 1–9, Plotinus explains that matter, the lowest level in his metaphysical hierarchy, does not even have being. There is a difficulty, in that case, about how the verb "to be" can be used of matter, or, to put it another way, about how we can say that matter "is." Whereas in Chapter 3 Plotinus appealed to the analysis of non-being in Plato's *Sophist*, here he talks in more Aristotelian terms, saying that "is" only applies to matter homonymously, that is, if we say that matter "is" and also that Intellect, for example, "is," then we are using the same word for two different things. Aristotle begins both *Metaphysics* 3.2 and *Metaphysics* 7.1 by stating that "things are said to be in many ways." In 3.2.1003a33–b10 he explains that "being" is like "health": both have more than one meaning but this is not a matter of chance; both have what is now called "focal meaning," in that the different senses all refer ultimately to one thing. In the case of health, some things preserve health (e.g., healthy food), others produce it (e.g., a healthy climate), others are a sign of it (e.g., a healthy complexion) and others possess it (e.g., healthy people). In *Nicomachean Ethics* 1.6.1096b25–29 he explains the range of meanings of the word "good" along similar lines. Aristotle distinguishes between this kind of "being said to be in many ways" and homonymy, where the same word is used for two completely different things (his example of the latter in *Categories* 1.1a1–6 is the Greek word *zōion* which can mean both "human being" and "picture"). Plotinus' notion of being is very different from Aristotle's and he uses the Aristotelian language of homonymy here in a way which blurs Aristotle's distinction between focal meaning and homonymy in order to express how it can be the case that matter both "is" and "is not."

5, 12–14 Plotinus repeats the general point that lack involves not being good, reiterates that total lack—as in matter—involves evil, and then alludes to the "great lack" which may be found in the individual soul that can fall into evil.

5, 14 *and is already evil. Accordingly, evil:* My translation here follows H-S_4, 306 in putting a full stop after *kakon* and starting a new sentence with *tōi* meaning "in this way," "accordingly."

5, 14–19 Once again Plotinus is keen to distinguish between evil in itself, generic evil, and specific evils in the soul such as particular vices. He sees the particular vices as species of vice in general, differentiated according to their objects (matter), soul parts (rational or irrational), and functions ("a sort of seeing" for the rational part and "impulse or experience" for the irrational part). The implied unity of the vices would be the obverse of the unity of the virtues discussed in Plato, *Protagoras* 328dff. and developed both within the Aristotelian tradition (see Alexander of Aphrodisias, *Supplement to On* *the Soul [De Anima Libri Mantissa]* 155.21–32 Bruns) and by the Stoics (see *SVF* I.200–201). (Cf. O'Meara [1999, 116–117] and Corrigan [1996b, 215–216].)

5, 19–23 Plotinus turns from moral to physical evil, setting out how in his view disease, ugliness, and poverty can all be explained as due to matter. His use of the conditional "if someone supposes that . . ." is worth noting: Like Plato in *Republic* 613a4–7, Plotinus holds that poverty and disease are not really evils for someone who is virtuous, a position he argues for in I.4.5–6 (see also III.2.5, 6–7). Deficiency and excess were mentioned in 4, 9 as features of evil in the irrational part of the soul (see Commentary 4, 6–12). Now these characteristics are applied to material bodies in a way which may owe something to medical ideas (cf. Galen, *Mixtures [De Temperamentis]* I.3 [I.521 Kuhn], *SVF* I.125 and 132, and Alexander of Aphrodisias, *Quaestiones* I.9.19.29–20.1.)

5, 23–24 *ugliness is matter not mastered by form*: Cf. the fuller account of the ugly offered in 1.6.2, 13–18.

5, 24–26 In 3, 16 Plotinus had described evil (matter) as "utter poverty;" now he describes poverty as want and privation due to the neediness of matter, using an unusual word for "neediness," *chrēsmosynē,* the word used in Heraclitus DK B65 to express the opposition between neediness and satiety (*koros*) at a cosmic level.

5, 26–34 The final lines of the chapter make clear that, although Plotinus holds that what is immaterial cannot be evil and regards matter as the source of evil, he also believes that not all beings with a material component are evil. To put it another way, his view is that matter is a necessary cause of evil but not a sufficient one. This is stated more explicitly in 14, 49–54 where it is clear that, for Plotinus, evil is produced by the combination of the soul and matter, not by either of these on its own (see Introduction 30–32 and Commentary 14, 49–54). For detailed discussion of Plotinus' position, with reference to 5, 30–34, see O'Brien (1971, 129–130), O'Brien (1993, 69–77) and, more briefly, O'Brien (1996, 185–187).

5, 28–30 These lines offer the first of two arguments for Plotinus' view, which he has just restated in lines 26–28, that evil has its origin not in the human soul but in matter. He appeals to the Socratic paradox found in Platonic dialogues such as the *Meno* and the *Gorgias*, that no one willingly does evil, as he had already done in 4, 11 (see Commentary 4, 6–12) and quotes Plato, *Phaedo* 107d1 on the possibility of escaping from evils. In the *Phaedo* passage the point is that virtue offers the only means of escape for the soul; Plotinus puts a positive spin on this by using the quotation to reinforce the possibility of such escape and so by implication arguing against Gnostic and Christian views which ascribe the responsibility for evil to human beings (see also II.9.12, 35–44 and cf. Origen, *On First Principles [De principiis]*

I.5.2–3, II.9.6). His remark that "not everyone is capable" raises the question of how much responsibility human beings ultimately have for their actions (cf. his discussion in III.2.10 of how to account for human moral responsibility in a world controlled by divine providence, and Introduction 33 and 38).

5, 30–34 In a second argument for the chapter's conclusion, Plotinus claims that it is not even the case that all material things contain evil: he has indicated in the previous sentence that not all human beings are evil and now he adds that "the perceptible gods," that is, the stars, are not. We can see from passages such as II.1.5, 18–19 and V.8.3, 27–28 that Plotinus takes it for granted that the stars are divine, a belief which was common in antiquity. (Festugière [1949–1954, II, 240–242] traces the belief back to Plato, *Laws* X 888e and 897c–899a and *Epinomis* 982aff.) In making the point here that the divinity of the stars exempts them from evil, Plotinus may be arguing against Numenius who thought that evil could be found in the heavenly bodies (see Numenius, fragment 52.115–121 des Places). He makes a similar point in arguing against the Gnostics in II.9.8, 30–36 and again in his criticisms of astrology in II.3.1, 6–10 and 17–19.

Chapter 6

In the first five chapters of the treatise Plotinus has set out the essentials of his answer to the questions posed in Chapter 1. Now he moves to supporting his answer by exegesis of Plato and to dealing with possible objections. In Chapters 6 and 7 he discusses Plato, Theaetetus *176a–177a in detail before turning to address possible objections in Chapters 8–15. In stating that evils do not exist among the gods, the passage of the* Theaetetus *confirms what Plotinus has just said in 5, 30–34 (see also Commentary 1, 1–2). The passage goes on to declare that evils are a necessary part of human life and describes the ethical ideal for human beings as* homoiōsis theōi *("becoming like God"). Plotinus examines it from a different point of view in I.2, his treatise* On Virtues, *where his focus is on how* homoiōsis theōi *should be understood. In this treatise, however, he is more concerned with the necessity of evils. Careful reading of* Theaetetus *176a5–9, in which Plato uses the word* hypenantion, *"opposite" or "contrary," leads to a discussion of the question whether there can be anything* enantion, *"contrary," to the Good, which draws on the account of contraries in Aristotle's* Categories *and*

Metaphysics. *Plotinus proceeds in a dialectical way, considering questions and objections that arise from the claim that evils necessarily exist and that there must be something contrary to the Good. He maintains that Plato is correct on both points, arguing for his own understanding of "contrary" which differs considerably from that of Aristotle. For detailed discussion of Plotinus' treatment of* homoiōsis theōi *both in I.2 and elsewhere, see Stern-Gillet (2019); for exposition of the complex argument in lines 31–59 see O'Brien (1996, 175–178) and Opsomer (2001, 181–182).*

6, 1–9 In *Theaetetus* 176a5–8 Socrates argues that evils are a necessary feature of life on earth because there must always be something contrary (*hypenantion*) to the good. Plotinus begins his exegesis of the passage by quoting much of it and arguing that it is consistent both with what he had said in 2, 25–32, about the absence of evil from the higher, divine levels of his metaphysical system, and with the view expressed in 5, 30–34, that the evil found in some human beings does not exist "among the perceptible gods," that is, the stars in the heavens. He offers a thoroughly Platonist reason for this latter view, namely the regularity of the movement of the heavens (see especially *Republic* 500c3–4 and cf. also *Timaeus* 47b–c). He expresses similar views in II.9.8, 30–36 and III.2.3, 28–31.

6, 9–13 Socrates' injunction at *Theaetetus* 176a9 to "escape from this place to that one as soon as possible" might suggest that readers are being encouraged to escape from life on earth into a heavenly realm. Plotinus takes a different view. The next sentence in the *Theaetetus* declares that "escape is becoming as like God as possible" and that this is a matter of "becoming just and pious with wisdom." Plotinus is therefore sticking closely to the text in pointing out that what Plato means is that we should try to escape from vice. The phrase *homoiōsis theōi,* "becoming like God," was one standard formulation of the aim of human life in Middle Platonism and was also popular with the Neoplatonists. The phrase is used in different ways by different thinkers. (For more details see Bonazzi [2007, 366–367], Boys-Stones [2018, 460–461, 465–466, 472–474].) For Plotinus, as we can see from passages such as I.2.1, 1–5 and I.6.8, 16–27, becoming like God means escaping from vice by turning the soul away from the physical world towards the divine realm from which it has descended. (Cf. Beierwaltes [1985, 24–31] on how Plotinus' understanding of turning away from the physical world differs from that of the Gnostics.)

6, 13–17 Plotinus goes back to Theodorus' remark at *Theaetetus* 176a2–4, that if Socrates persuaded everyone of his views, there would be more peace and less evil on earth. In Plato's text it is Socrates who takes Theodorus to be suggesting that evils might come to an end and who responds that evils exist of necessity because "there must be something contrary to the good." Plotinus follows Plato in holding that evils necessarily exist but the talk of "something contrary to the good" is problematic for him as it might seem to suggest a dualist metaphysics in which absolute evil is opposed to absolute good. In the rest of the chapter he uses Aristotelian terminology as a tool with which to explain his understanding of "contrary" here.

6, 17–21 Plotinus begins his discussion of the question whether there is something contrary to the good by remarking that vice in human beings, which is only a secondary evil, is contrary not to the Good but to human moral virtue. The idea that such virtue makes it possible to master matter is repeated from 5, 26–34. In making the point in line 21 that the Good "has no quality" (*ou . . . poion*) Plotinus is starting to draw on Aristotle's discussion of contraries in the *Categories.* In *Categories* 5.3b24–4b19 Aristotle argues that substances (*ousiai*) admit contrary qualities, but have nothing contrary to them; in *Metaphysics* 14.1.1087b2–3 he repeats the point that substance has no contrary, in a context where he is arguing against philosophers who make their first principles contraries. Although Plotinus will argue later in this chapter that there can be a contrary to substance as such, at this stage he appears happy to take from Aristotle an initial argument that there is no contrary to the Good because the category of quality does not apply to it. Similarly, in VI.9.3, 36–44 Plotinus argues that various categories, including quality and quantity, do not apply to the One (cf. Meijer [1992, 129–134]).

6, 21–27 Plotinus moves to a further question about the claim in the *Theaetetus* that "there must be something contrary to the good." He turns to a different passage of Aristotle's *Categories*, 11.14a6–10, and picks up on the point made there, that one of a pair of contraries can exist without the other. He responds to this by suggesting that the statement in the *Theaetetus* is meant to apply only to the Good, not to contraries in general, a suggestion which is not developed here, but which he will return to in Chapter 7.

6, 27–30 Plotinus returns to Aristotle's argument in *Categories* 5.3b24–4b19 that substances do not have contraries, and presents it from his own rather different perspective. Plotinus' highest principle, the Good, is not a substance or being (*ousia*), but, like the Form of the Good in Plato, *Republic* 509b, is "beyond substance/being." In saying "That there is nothing contrary to substance has been reliably proved by induction in the case of particular substances" Plotinus accepts Aristotle's argument to some extent, while reading Aristotle from the perspective of a Platonist. In *Categories* 5.3b25–27 Aristotle is explicit about what he means by "a primary substance" in this context, saying ". . . there is nothing contrary to an individual man, nor yet is there anything contrary to man or to animal." Elsewhere in Aristotle *ousiai*, "substances" or "beings," are primarily individual things. By contrast, for Plotinus, as for Plato, *ousia*, "being," is primarily a feature of the intelligible world. (These different conceptions of *ousia* make this chapter particularly difficult to translate, since "substance" is a standard English translation for *ousia* in Aristotle's sense, while in Platonist contexts the word is more often translated as "being.") We have already seen Plotinus moving between Platonic and Aristotelian discussions of *ousia* in 3, 1–9, 3, 16–24, and 5, 9–12. Here he uses Aristotle's argument that there is nothing contrary to substance in a very un-Aristotelian context as he attempts to make sense of the claim in the *Theaetetus* that "there is something contrary to the good."

6, 31–38 Plotinus presents his own understanding of "contrary," according to which "non-substance" is the contrary of "substance" (or, in Platonist language, "non-being" is the contrary of "being") and evil, as a whole, is the contrary of good, as a whole. Aristotle in *Categories* 11.14a15–16 states that "It is clearly the nature of contraries to belong to the same thing (the same either in species or in genus)"; in that sense, according to Plotinus, they have something in common. Plotinus contrasts the sense in which "wholes" such as the principle of good and the principle of evil are contraries with this, when he declares that "the wholes . . . are more contrary to each other than the rest."

6, 39–47 Plotinus quotes part of the statement at Aristotle, *Categories* 6.6a17–18 that "contraries are the furthest apart from each other" and uses it to argue that good and evil have contrary characteristics, including those of truth and falsehood. It is worth noting that in Aristotle's text this statement is attributed to people who hold views (about the category of quantity) that Aristotle does not himself subscribe to; moreover, it includes a crucial rider which Plotinus omits. Where the *Categories* says "contraries are the furthest apart from each other within the same genus," Plotinus allows contraries simply to be "the furthest apart from each other" even if they are not in the same genus. The contrast between lack of limit and lack of measure, as characteristics of evil, and limit and measure as characteristics of good recalls 3, 12–18.

6, 41–43 *Indeed, lack of . . . divine nature contains*: The manuscripts of Plotinus have the words *ta alla* twice in these lines, once in line 41 and again in lines 42–43. The words do not fit into the grammar of the sentence the first time and accordingly I follow Dodds (1965, 420) and H-S$_4$, 307 in treating them as a copyist's error which does not belong in the text; if they were included the translation would read ". . .lack of limit, lack of measure and all the other characteristics which the evil nature has are contrary to limit, measure and all the other characteristics which the divine nature contains."

6, 44–47 *And the evil . . . of the divine*: My translation here follows H-S_2 rather than H-S_4, reading *to kat'ousian* ("the being [of the evil nature]") rather than *to <mē> kat'ousian* ("the non-being"). I agree with O'Meara (1999, 69–70n39) and Narbonne (2001, 122n1) that the addition of *mē*, although based on Simplicius, *Commentary on the Categories* 110.13–14, is not appropriate to Plotinus' argument here.

6, 47–54 Fire and water are regarded by Aristotle as "simple bodies" which have contrary qualities (see *On Generation and Corruption* 2.3). Plotinus takes a different view: if fire and water were distinct substances, he would be prepared to say that they were contraries in themselves, but in fact both fire and water are constituted by matter, which takes on the contrary qualities of hot and dry, wet and cold, to form fire and water respectively.

6, 54–59 Plotinus ends the chapter with his own definition of what it is for one thing to be contrary to another. His statement that "contrariety does not depend on quality or, in general, on any particular category of being" reiterates his disagreement with the way in which Aristotle had defined contrariety in terms of his doctrine of categories. Plotinus' own definition of contrariety allows him to accept the statement made in the *Theaetetus* that there is something contrary to the Good.

6, 58 *opposing elements*: In *Categories* 10 Aristotle lists contraries as one of four ways in which things can be opposed to one another (*antikeisthai*). Plotinus' mention of "opposing elements" (*antitheta*) here may be an allusion to this, but he is not equating contrariety with Aristotle's notion of opposition (cf. O'Meara [1999, 128–129]).

Chapter 7

In this chapter Plotinus takes a different approach to the question of the necessity of evil raised by Theaetetus *176a–177a. Following the suggestion in 6, 25–27 that the statement that "there must be something contrary to the Good" applies only to the Good rather than to contraries in general, he appeals to passages from other Platonic dialogues to elucidate the* Theaetetus, *and then argues on metaphysical grounds that there must be a final stage to procession from the One.*

7, 1–7 Plotinus considers a different argument for the necessity of evil from those discussed in Chapter 6, namely that the All, by which he means the physical universe, necessarily contains matter and contraries. The mention of contraries provides a link to the arguments of the previous chapter, although here Plotinus is speaking of contraries simply in the Aristotelian sense. He supports his argument by quoting *Timaeus* 47e5–48a1 ("the nature of this universe is a mixture of intellect and necessity") and adapting a phrase from *Politicus* 273b5 ("the ancient nature"). The idea that everything which comes to the universe from God is good, a very important idea for Plotinus, is also derived from the *Timaeus,* from passages such as 28a–29b.

In appealing to these passages from the *Timaeus* and the *Politicus,* Plotinus implies an interpretation of the *Timaeus* according to which the mention of "necessity" in *Timaeus* 47e5–48a1 points forward to the "receptacle" of 49a6, and that receptacle is understood as matter; he also implies an interpretation of the *Politicus* according to which the "ancient nature" of 273b5 is likewise understood as matter. He interprets *Timaeus* 47e5–48a1 along similar lines in III.2.2, 31–42. These interpretations were already controversial in antiquity and remain so in modern scholarship: Proclus in *On the Existence of Evils* 32 criticizes Plotinus' interpretation of the *Timaeus,* as discussed in the Introduction, 37. O'Meara (1999, 33 and 130–131), following Hager (1977, 460–461), regards Proclus' interpretation of the *Timaeus* as "Aristotelizing" and Plotinus' view as closer to Plato's, while Opsomer (2001, 179–180) agrees with this view of Proclus, but is not so sure that Plotinus' conception of matter is more Platonic, querying Plotinus' identification of matter with the "refractory element" associated with the receptacle in the *Timaeus.* In general, Plotinus reads *Theaetetus, Timaeus,* and *Politicus* as all supporting his view that matter is the source of evil and a necessary component of the universe: his exegesis of Plato goes hand-in-hand with his understanding of cosmology, although the latter is also supported by philosophical arguments independent of his exegesis.

7, 7–12 Plotinus returns to *Theaetetus* 176a–177a and explicates further details of the passage by appealing to another passage of the *Timaeus*, 41b2–4, in which the demiurge addresses the younger gods who are responsible for producing the mortal bodies of human beings and combining these with the individual immortal souls produced by the demiurge. Taken literally, this passage states that, although the younger gods were generated, they are nevertheless everlasting and will never be destroyed. However Plotinus does not take the passage literally as we can see from V.8.12, 20–25; rather, he holds that talk of the younger gods or the physical universe being generated by the demiurge should be understood as a way of expressing their atemporal dependence on the intelligible. Accordingly, he reads this second *Timaeus* passage as supporting the claim made by Socrates in the *Theaetetus* that evils will never be destroyed and so confirming the necessity of evil.

7, 7 *What does he mean . . .* : I have not translated the words *ei theōito* at the beginning of this sentence which are printed in square brackets in H-S_2. They make no sense as they stand and may derive from an explanatory gloss such as *en Theaetētōi* "in the *Theaetetus*," as suggested by Sleeman (1937, 225). An alternative, followed in H-S_1 and in several translations, including Armstrong (1966, 296–297) and Gerson (2018, 117), would be to adopt Engelhardt and Creuzer's emendation, to read *ek theou tou* and attach the phrase to the end of the previous sentence, translating the latter part of that as "the underlying matter that has not yet been ordered by some god." This would fit the allusion there to *Politicus* 273b, but would be extremely awkward Greek.

7, 12–16 Plotinus concludes his exposition of the *Theaetetus* passage by returning to the interpretation of "escape" which he had argued for in the previous chapter. In understanding acquisition of virtue as separating oneself from the body, he clearly has in mind passages of the *Phaedo* such as 66d7–67d2, although he contents himself with a vague reference to "somewhere" in Plato rather than quoting the text, perhaps because this is his own standard doctrine, also found in I.2 as well as in II.3.9, 20, III.6.5, 13–19 and V.1.10, 24–27. Plotinus is careful here to distinguish between the body and matter (cf. 4, 1–6 and Commentary 4, 1–6).

7, 15–16 *being "among the gods"... these are immortal*: Here Plotinus adds in a quick interpretation of the phrase "among the gods" found in *Theaetetus* 176a7, taking this to refer to the intelligible gods who are immortal and immaterial, although 6, 1–9 implies that the reference is to the perceptible gods mentioned in 5, 30–34 (see Commentary 5, 30–34). It seems that considering the *Theaetetus* passage alongside *Timaeus* 41b and reminiscences of the *Phaedo* has pulled Plotinus in a different interpretative direction from that taken at the end of Chapter 5 and the beginning of Chapter 6. This shift of viewpoint makes clear that, although Plotinus is using exegesis of Plato to support his argument, he is more concerned to offer a philosophical response to the question of the nature and source of evils than to comment on any specific passage of Plato.

7, 16–23 In the final lines of the chapter Plotinus offers a metaphysical argument for the necessity of evil, declaring that procession from the Good, as the highest principle, must come to an end at a final point from which good is completely absent and labelling this final point "matter." One might expect from the metaphysics expounded in Chapter 2 that the lowest level of emanation from the Good would be something deficient in good, rather than something specifically evil. In III.2.5, 25–32 Plotinus explains the claim in *Theaetetus* 176a that evils cannot be destroyed in just these terms, although he also alludes in III.2.5, 27 to something other than good which is responsible for the deficiency. Here in I.8 Plotinus has a lot more to say about what that something might be. At the beginning of Chapter 3 he stated that evil is not "situated among the things that are" and went on to argue that it belongs "among the things that are not." In Chapter 6 he went further and argued that evil is the contrary of the Good. Now he argues that this contrary is the final point of a series emanating from the first principle. It is not obvious why such a series has to be finite or why its "last item" must be evil. The argument was subjected to rigorous criticism by Proclus, as mentioned in the Introduction, 35, and has been carefully examined in modern scholarship: see especially O'Meara (1998) and O'Meara (2005).

Chapter 8

In this chapter Plotinus moves to considering objections to his view that matter is the origin of evil. Discussion of such objections will occupy him for the rest of the treatise, although in Chapter 9 he turns aside to discuss how we can know evil, a question raised in Chapter 1 but not yet addressed in detail. He starts with two, related objections both of which address the problem of moral evil. According to the first objection, ignorance and wicked desires are due not to matter but to the combination of matter and form in the body. Plotinus responds to this by outlining his theory of how form and matter interact within the body, arguing that, once they have entered into matter, forms become corrupted and infected; the ultimate responsibility thus rests with matter as the source of infection. The second objection then appears as a reply to Plotinus' response, declaring that "matter should be mastered," the implication being that matter alone cannot be responsible for moral evil. He responds to this further objection by emphasizing the power of matter to destabilize the desires and thoughts of human beings. He concludes the chapter by re-affirming his view that moral evil is secondary evil and that it is matter which is primary evil.

8, 1–10 In this paragraph Plotinus formulates the first objection to be considered. This objection concedes that ignorance and wicked desires are not due to the soul, but suggests that they are a result of form producing particular bodily humors and of the wrong kind of "fillings" and "emptyings." Plotinus seems to have several different passages of Plato in mind here: a theory of humors of the kind he sketches can be found in *Timaeus* 86e–87a, while pleasures and desires are described as fillings and emptyings in *Republic* IX.584b–585e, *Timaeus* 65a and *Philebus* 35b and 42c–d (cf. also *Republic* IV.439d). According to the theory of humors in the *Timaeus*, dispositions such as irritability and despondency, vices such as rashness and cowardice, and intellectual failings such as forgetfulness and being slow to learn are all the result of acid, salty phlegm and bitter, bilious humors becoming trapped in the body and mingling with the movement of the soul, while according to *Republic* IX and *Philebus* 42c–d, those who satisfy their desires by filling themselves with knowledge and virtue will experience true pleasures and will be much happier than those who satisfy only their bodily desires. Plotinus presents the objection as hypothetical, but it is tempting to see here a reflection of argument within his school over the interpretation of these Platonic passages and their implications for the understanding of evil. Plotinus' response to the objection, in the next paragraph, explains his view of how bodily humors are produced without addressing the talk of fillings and emptyings. The latter, however, reappears later in the chapter when he responds to the claim that matter should be mastered.

8, 10–13 Plotinus makes two points in reply to the objection. The first, already implied in 4, 14–17, is that forms in matter require matter for their effectiveness. To support this, he appeals to Aristotle's example of the axe in *On the Soul (De Anima)* 2.1.412b12 and *Parts of Animals* 1.642a10–11. Aristotle's point in *On the Soul* is that it is the axe-shape which makes an axe what it is and not just a lump of iron; the example illustrates the relationship of soul and body, which for him is comparable to that of form and matter. Plotinus uses the example in this way in I.1.4, 20–23, although his understanding of how form and matter combine is quite different from Aristotle's. In *Parts of Animals* Aristotle's point is more like that made by Plotinus here, that for the axe to perform its function of splitting things, it must be made of a particular kind of material, either bronze or iron.

8, 13–24 Plotinus presents the second point in his reply to the objection, which follows on from the first one: on the one hand forms are ineffective without matter, but on the other matter has a bad influence on them. The first point makes matter a necessary condition of evils such as ignorance and wicked desires, while the second clarifies that matter, by corrupting and infecting enmattered forms, operates as a cause of such evils. The metaphor of "infection," derived from *Phaedo* 67a4–5, has already been used in 4, 22 (see Commentary 4, 17–22). In developing this second point, Plotinus uses the distinctive notion of "contrary" which he had expounded in Chapter 6, speaking of matter "applying its contrary nature to form" and "opposing its formlessness to the form of heat" as well as the description of evil as formless and unmeasured which he had used in 3, 12–20.

8, 17–19 *Not even fire . . . are in matter*: O'Meara (1999, 74) proposes moving this sentence and placing it a few lines earlier on the grounds that it fits better with the first point in Plotinus' reply than with the second. He suggests that the sentence has been omitted at some stage in the copying of the text and then put back in not quite the right place. The paragraph would then read: "Even someone who says this will nonetheless be forced to concede that matter is evil. For the quality in matter does not do what it does when it is separate. Not even fire burns by itself, nor do any other things by themselves produce what they are said to do when they are in matter, just as the shape of the axe does not do anything without the iron. Then too the forms in matter are not the same as they would be if they existed on their own; as material principles they are corrupted in matter and are infected with its nature. For matter takes control of what is manifested in it and corrupts and destroys it . . ." Kalligas (2014, 236) argues against this, seeing fire as an illustrative example of the second point in Plotinus' reply. On balance, the case for moving the sentence does not seem to me strong enough to justify making the change.

8, 24–28 Plotinus supplements the second point of his reply to the objection under consideration by comparing the way in which forms are changed by becoming enmattered with the way in which the characteristics of an animal's food are changed in the process of digestion. He then concludes that the objection in fact implies that matter is responsible for evil. The account of digestion used by Plotinus here can also be found in Porphyry, Fr. 259F.90–99 = Nemesius *On the Nature of Man* 3.39.20–40.1 where a similar comparison is made and explicitly ascribed to Ammonius Saccas, the teacher of Plotinus. The account may derive from the discussion of nutrition in Aristotle, *On the Soul* 2.4.416a30–416b9.

8, 26–27 *all the humors . . . that receives them*: In translating these words I follow H-S_4, 307 and most other recent editors and translators in reading the neuter plural pronoun *haper* in line 26 rather than *hyper*, the word found in the manuscripts, which makes no evident sense, or the masculine plural pronoun, *hoiper*, suggested by Sleeman (1926, 152). *Hoiper* would refer to the humors, so that the translation would read "all the humors become those which belong to the animal that receives them."

8, 28–37 The second objection, following on from Plotinus' response to the first one, implies that the soul should be able to resist the influence of matter. Plotinus here takes a rather pessimistic view of this possibility, using the understanding of "escape" based on the *Phaedo* which he had already used in 6, 9–13 and 7, 12–14 to argue that both desires and judgements are affected by our bodily state. This is consistent with the contrast drawn in Chapter 4 between the damaged state of the soul which has entered into matter and the perfection and purity of the soul which "inclines towards Intellect." A similar account of the way in which diseases of the soul are due to the disposition of the body can be found in *Timaeus* 86b–87a, the passage within which the theory of humors used in formulating the first objection appears, while the reference to the difference in our desires and thoughts between when we are full and when we are empty may be another allusion to the talk of "fillings" and "emptyings" at *Republic* IV.439d, *Republic* IX.584b–585e, *Timaeus* 65a, and *Philebus* 35b and 42c–d, again as in the formulation of the first objection (cf. also *Timaeus* 43a–b). The *Timaeus'* view of the effect of the body on the soul is similarly reflected in Galen's treatise, *The Capacities of the Soul Depend on the Mixtures of the Body* (see Galen, *Psychological Writings* [2013, 335–428] for a discussion and translation of this text).

One might suppose from what Plotinus says in this passage that he regards all vice as due to matter and absolves the soul from any responsibility for moral evil. However, his view is more complex than this, as he has already indicated in 4, 12–15, 19, and will explain more fully in 14, 27–49 and 15, 12–23. (Cf. Introduction 30–34, Commentary 4, 17–22, 14, 25–37, 14, 38–43, 15, 12–23.)

8, 37–44 In the last paragraph of the chapter Plotinus repeats ideas already argued for in 3, 39–4, 5, implying that he has refuted the two objections raised and so confirmed the correctness of his earlier analysis. The objections under consideration in this chapter focus more on whether matter is indeed primary evil than on the point that vice is only secondary evil. Plotinus' re-introduction of this latter point indicates his own concern with the problem of moral evil. That problem is at best implicit in the objections, but in considering them Plotinus is also working towards the discussion of the soul's role in moral evil which he will develop in Chapters 14 and 15.

8, 40–41 *In the same way . . . dark is secondary*: This sentence picks up the imagery used in 4, 17–5, 5, comparing primary evil, matter, to darkness and secondary evil to that which is darkened (see Commentary 4, 17–22, 4, 25–32).

Chapter 9

Before he goes on to consider further objections to his view that matter is evil, Plotinus in this chapter addresses the issue of how we can know evil that was raised in 1, 7–17. The question is treated again, more briefly, in 13, 14–20. Its discussion here has been criticized as an awkward insertion (e.g., by O'Meara [1999, 141]) but should be understood in the light of Plotinus' concern throughout the treatise with the explanation of moral evil, as mentioned above (Commentary 8, 37–44). Any suggestion that the soul can recognize evil might be thought to imply that there is some kind of evil inherent in the soul, a position which Plotinus consistently argues against. He therefore in this chapter seeks to find another way of describing how we can come to an understanding of evil, once again using the analogy of "seeing" darkness which he had already used in 4, 17–5, 5 and had picked up in 8, 40–41.

9, 1 *With what, then, do we know these evils?:* A literal translation of this sentence would be "With what, then, do we know these?" Many translators have understood "these" to refer to "good and evil" but since the discussion which follows is only concerned with our knowledge of evil, I have followed O'Meara (1999, 75) in taking "these" to refer to "evils." The chapter then proceeds to discuss our knowledge of both secondary and primary evil, following the mention of both types of evil in 8, 37–44.

9, 2–3 The statement that we know virtue by intellect and by the intellectual virtue of wisdom picks up the claim in 1, 8 that "understanding of each thing comes by likeness." All the ancient philosophical schools treated wisdom as one of the virtues and from the time of Aristotle onwards, the word used to refer to this virtue was the one Plotinus uses, *phronēsis.* Here, as suggested by Blumenthal (1993, IX, 278n14), Plotinus may be using the word in the specific sense defined in I.6.6, 12–13: "wisdom is an intellectual activity which turns away from the things below and leads the soul to those above."

9, 3–4 The analogy with the ruler (*kanōn*) recalls Aristotle, *On the Soul* 1.5.411a5–7, where Aristotle makes the point that we use a straight ruler to know both the straight and the crooked. Plotinus uses the same analogy in I.6.3, 5 and V.3.3, 6–12. Here, however, he is dissatisfied with the easy answer that we can tell what does not fit with virtue and presses for an answer in terms of whether we can actually see, or look at, vice. On Plotinus' use of both *kanōn* and *epharmozō* ("fit with") in a number of passages, including this one, see Blumenthal (1993, IX, 258–264).

I have followed H-S_2 in treating the word *kakian* ("vice"), in line 4 as an explanatory gloss and so have not translated it.

9, 5–11 To answer his own question Plotinus makes a distinction between absolute and partial vice which recalls the distinction made in 5, 14–19 between "wickedness in the soul" and its various species which are "formed by additions" (see Commentary 5, 14–19). He also appeals to the idea of "lack" used earlier, especially in 5, 1–14, and now states that we cannot see absolute, unlimited vice, but can only know it by abstraction. Elsewhere Plotinus uses these notions of addition and abstraction when he is attempting to describe how to approach the One: see V.5.13, 9–12 and VI.7.36, 7; here he makes the radical move of using them to describe how we can come to some understanding of absolute vice and, in the next paragraph, of matter.

9, 11–14 Plotinus compares the way in which we know partial vice, recognizing its lack of virtue, with the way in which we identify ugliness, acknowledging the lack of form which would make a face, for example, beautiful; this is the same account of ugliness as in I.6.2, 16–18. The phrase "rational principle" translates the Greek word *logos*, used by Plotinus to refer to the formative principles which make individual physical things what they are: for a brief discussion of Plotinus' theory of the *logos*, with further references, see Corrigan (1996a, 110–112).

9, 14–18 Plotinus turns from secondary to primary evil and attempts to explain how we can arrive at a conception of matter. We again do this by abstraction, as was already implied in earlier passages such as 3, 12–16. For Plotinus, as for Numenius in fragment 52, 121–127, matter is simply that in which there is no form. The use of the verb *emellomen*, in line 17 ("if we are going to look at matter") suggests that the movement of abstraction described in these lines is voluntary, although, since such abstraction enables us to know evil only indirectly, it is less potentially dangerous than the experience of "seeing and not seeing" described in the lines which follow. Similarly, in II.4.10, 13–19 abstraction is the first of two ways in which we can come to some understanding of matter (cf. also II.4.12, 28–34 and see below Commentary 9, 18–26.)

9, 15–16 *Completely abstracting all . . . is no form*: I follow H-S$_4$, 307 in reading *to parapan <pan> eidos aphairountes, hōi mē tauta paresti*, treating the repetition of *pan eidos* after *aphairountes* as an explanatory gloss which should be deleted.

9, 18–26 Plotinus turns now to describing a more direct experience of evil by the fallen soul as a kind of blinding. The distinction between this and the indirect knowledge of evil gained through abstraction which was mentioned in 9, 14–18 is well set out by O'Meara (1999, 144–146); he draws attention to a similar shift in II.4.10 to the language of experience, rather than knowledge, in II.4.10, 20–21 and 34–35 and goes so far as to suggest that the soul's experience of matter is a "counter-ecstasy," diametrically opposed to the mystical experience of the One, but structurally comparable to it insofar as it lies beyond the realm of the intelligible.

Plotinus appeals, as he had already done at the end of Chapter 4, to the imagery of light and darkness to explain how intellect can "see" matter: it is like seeing darkness, which we can only do if we turn away from the light (see Commentary 4, 25–32). Matter is similarly described as "dark" and "beneath the light" in II.4.5, 7–12 (cf. the comments on that passage in Long [2016, 46]). Plotinus emphasizes that, in behaving like this, intellect is going against its own nature, "going forth outside itself" and "going to what does not belong to it." As in Chapter 6, Plotinus talks in terms of contraries, but, whereas there he described evil as contrary to the Good, this time he describes matter as contrary to intellect because it is contrary to form. While the analogy with seeing darkness is striking and to some degree effective, whether Plotinus has really given a satisfactory answer to the question at the beginning of the chapter remains a moot point.

9, 18–19 *For this reason . . . belong to it*: Plotinus calls the faculty by which we can "see" matter "another intellect," using language similar to that used in II.4.10, 1–11 where he refers explicitly to the "bastard reasoning" of Plato, *Timaeus* 52b, which according to Timaeus' account is the faculty by which we apprehend "space" (*chōra*). It is notable that Plotinus describes this "other intellect" as "daring" (*tolmēsas*), suggesting a greater, and riskier, degree of voluntariness than was involved in the movement of abstraction described immediately above. However, Corrigan (1996b, 224) seems to me mistaken in suggesting that there is anything new about the way in which Plotinus is using the language of *tolmā* ("daring") here; Plotinus' use of this language and its connection with "the awkward problem of the descent of the soul" is well discussed in Atkinson (1983, 4–6).

9, 21–22 *Without this it cannot see*: I follow Dodds as reported in the *apparatus criticus* of H-S_2, O'Meara (1999, 53 and 76) and others in reading *toutou* ("this"), rather than *tou* ("something") in line 21.

Chapter 10

In this short chapter Plotinus returns to considering objections to his thesis that matter is evil. In the previous chapter he had sought to avoid implying that evil is inherent in the soul as he wrestled with attempting to describe how we can come to an understanding of evil. The objection to which he now turns, that matter cannot be evil because it has no qualities, appears in Plutarch, On the Generation of the Soul in the Timaeus *6.1014E–1015B, as part of an argument for the principle of evil being an irrational, maleficent soul. This is precisely the view which Plotinus is concerned to argue against throughout the treatise and so it should be no surprise that he moves from discussion of how we can know evil to consideration of this particular objection. Plotinus does hold that matter has no qualities (cf. II.4.8, 1–3 and 13, 7–28) but argues that matter has a nature which is evil in a non-qualitative sense. The relationship between Plotinus' view of matter, particularly in II.4, and the notions of matter found in earlier Greek philosophers is clearly set out in Long (2016) and Long (2022, 18–29).*

10, 1–6 The characterization of matter as "without quality" (*apoios*) is Stoic (see *SVF* I.85 = Diogenes Laertius 7.134) while the reference to matter "receiving" qualities is Platonic (see *Timaeus* 50b6; cf. also 51a7), and the use of the term "substrate" (*hypokeimenon)* is Aristotelian. (See Aristotle, *Metaphysics* 1.3.983a30, 7.3.1029a1–5, 7.13.1038b5, 8.1.1042a26–31. Cf. also Aristotle, *On the Heavens [De Caelo]* 3.8.306b17.) The same combination of terminology used by different philosophical schools in the discussion of matter is already present in Plutarch, *On the Generation of the Soul in the Timaeus* 1014E–1015B and in other Middle Platonist authors (cf. Plutarch, *Moralia XIII, part 1* [1976, 188–190], Dillon [1993, 89–92]). In 9, 14–16 Plotinus had described matter in more purely Platonist language as "that in which there is no form." Here he introduces the idea that matter has "some nature" (line 5); in 10, 15–16, he will combine the Platonist language of Chapter 9 with his own, distinctive notion of "contrary" developed in Chapter 6 and describe the evil, non-qualitative nature of matter as "a nature contrary to form."

10, 6–11 Plotinus' statement that "Quality is that in virtue of which something else is said to be qualified" echoes Aristotle, *Categories* 8.8b25, and he is again using Aristotelian language in describing quality as "accidental" (cf., e.g., Aristotle, *Posterior Analytics* 1.4.73b3–5, *Topics* 1.5.102b4ff.). However, Plotinus' understanding of quality is rather different from

Aristotle's. In II.6 Plotinus criticizes Aristotle's notion of quality and concludes "That, then, which is never a form of something else but always an accidental attribute, this and only this is pure quality" (II.6.3, 28–29). He is using "quality" here in that restricted sense.

10, 11–12 Plotinus adds an additional argument for matter being without quality, that to ascribe quality to matter would be to make the same kind of mistake as ascribing quality to quality itself, to the Form of quality. The point that quality itself is without quality appears in a similar context in II.4.13, 19, where Plotinus is arguing that matter is not quality.

10, 12–16 Plotinus ends the chapter by reiterating that matter is evil precisely because it lacks quality, just as it lacks form. In 6, 31–59 he had argued that matter is contrary to substance. Now he describes it as contrary to form. (On the connection between these two claims, cf. O'Brien [1996, 176 and 184].)

Chapter 11

Plotinus now considers a further objection to his view that matter is evil. According to this objection, if evil consists in privation, it will always be in something else, and evil in the soul will not be due to anything external. This objection thus presents another threat to Plotinus' view that there is no evil inherent in the soul. To counter it, Plotinus uses ideas from Plato's Phaedo *and* Republic, *arguing that the soul is, of its nature, both alive and good; it follows that the soul cannot be primary evil nor can such evil be an accident of it. For a clear summary of the argument of this chapter, and its connection with the* Phaedo, *see O'Brien (1996, 184–185).*

11, 1–6 Plotinus sets out the argument to which he will respond in the second half of the chapter. The opening words build on Plotinus' own description of matter in 10, 15–16 as "a nature contrary to form." Plotinus repeats this here, adding the definite article and the word "all" so that matter is now said to be "the nature contrary to all form;" this is then equated with the Aristotelian concept of privation (see Aristotle, *Physics* 1.7.190b24–27 and 9.192a3–6). The objection applies this concept to evil, arguing that if evil consists in privation, then there is no such thing as evil in itself, and so evil in the soul is due simply to privation within the soul.

11, 6–9 It now appears that Plotinus in this chapter is dealing not so much with a single objection as with a family of objections, some of which draw the conclusion that there is no such thing as matter (a view to which Plotinus returns at 15, 1–3) while others hold that matter exists but is not evil (which was also the view discussed in Chapter 10). Either way, the origin of evil will then lie in the soul. Plotinus' response to these objections focuses on this conclusion, which he regards as a contradiction in terms.

11, 10–19 Plotinus responds to the objection by using an argument from Plato's *Phaedo* combined with ideas which derive ultimately from Plato's *Republic*. I take the words "by the operation of its own principle" in line 12 to refer to the operation of a principle (*logos*) within the soul, referred to again in line 15 with the words "It has life by its own principle": cf. O'Meara (1999, 78n62). Because the Greek word *psychē*, "soul," can refer simply to a principle of life, Plato in *Phaedo* 102a10–107a1 argues that the soul is essentially, by definition, alive and so cannot die (see especially 105d and cf. Plotinus IV.7.2, 5–6); according to this argument it is contradictory to speak of a "dead soul." Plotinus argues that the soul is also essentially good, in which case it is equally contradictory to speak of an "evil soul"; soul can be evil only in a secondary sense. In Plotinus' view, the soul cannot be deprived of good, but must be "of a good kind." because of its origins in Intellect.

The claim that both life and goodness are essential characteristics of the soul goes back to Plato, *Republic* I 352e–353e. (Cf. also *Republic* X 608e–611a. Plotinus would naturally have connected Plato's use of the verb *steresthai*, "to be deprived of" at *Republic* I 353c9 and e2 with the noun *sterēsis*, "privation.") The word *agathoeides*, "of a good kind," comes from Plato *Republic* VI 509a3 and appears numerous times in Plotinus' full discussion of the relationship between the life of Intellect and the Good in VI.7.15–22.

Chapter 12

This very short chapter goes closely with the preceding one. Plotinus considers a further objection which belongs to the same family of objections as those considered in Chapter 11, that evil in the soul is "a partial privation of good." In reply, he argues that any such evil would not be primary evil, as it would not be unmixed.

12, 5–7 *Also the soul . . . sort of accident*: This is another way of making the point about the essential goodness of soul that was made in Chapter 11; the admission that evil will be present in the soul "as some sort of accident" might seem to contradict what was affirmed in 11, 17–19, but the point now is that such evil is secondary, rather than primary, evil. Once again, Plotinus is concerned to argue against any theory which places the origin of evil in the soul.

Chapter 13

In this chapter Plotinus addresses another objection which, like the previous ones, would make the soul responsible for evil. According to this objection evil is "an impediment" which produces evil within the soul. Plotinus responds that such an impediment would itself be the product of something external to the soul. He reiterates that vice—which might be described as an impediment of this kind—is only a secondary evil, just as virtue is only a secondary good. In extreme cases, however, the soul may descend so completely into evil that it can no longer be called a soul at all. At the end of the chapter Plotinus adduces texts from Plato which support this way of talking about the "death" of the fallen soul.

13, 1–2 *Then perhaps the soul . . . eye in seeing*: There are difficulties over both the Greek text of this sentence and its interpretation. I follow the text of H-S_2 and the interpretation given in the *apparatus criticus* to that text, according to which the pronoun *toutōi*, "this," refers to the soul. Plotinus seems still to have in mind *Republic* I 352e–353e mentioned above (Commentary 11, 10–19). In that passage the eyes are a key example of something which cannot perform its function well if it is not in a good state. See 353b–c and cf. also *Alcibiades* I 126b, *Laches* 190a, and Denyer's remark in his edition of Plato, *Alcibiades* (2001, 201): "the way that eyes are the better for the presence of sight is Plato's favourite illustration of how a thing is the better for the presence of the virtue proper to it." As I understand it, the objection, which is somewhat telegraphically expressed by Plotinus, uses Plato's own example of the eyes and compares evil in the soul to a sight defect: just as such a defect can prevent the eye from performing its proper function of seeing, so evil can prevent the soul from performing its proper function which, for a Platonist, is living well; Plotinus uses the example in a similar way in I.7.3, 2–3.

13, 2–4 *But in that case . . . is something different*: Plotinus responds briskly that an impediment of the kind suggested in the objection would not be evil itself. It is not clear who or what is referred to by the word *autois* in this sentence. I follow O'Meara (1999, 79 and 152) in taking it as a reference to the proponents of the objection, and so translate it as "in their view."

13, 4–14 It now becomes clear that it is vice which the objection posits as an "impediment" in the soul. Plotinus can answer that easily enough by appealing to the account of moral evil offered at the end of Chapter 8. For a detailed discussion of this passage and of Proclus' implicit criticisms of it in *On the Existence of Evils* 47 and 50, see O'Meara (1998, IX, 1–15).

13, 14–26 The talk in lines 13–14 of how we can descend from vice to evil itself leads Plotinus to expatiate on the horrors of such a fall, drawing on imagery taken from a variety of passages in Plato. "The place of unlikeness" is a reference to *Politicus* 273d6–e1 (where Plotinus read *topon*, "place," as in our manuscripts of Plato; the reading *ponton*, "sea," preferred by modern editors, is a correction by Proclus). The metaphor of "falling into dark mud," followed by the description of soul as sinking in matter until it is able to stir and "lift its gaze from the mud," echoes both *Phaedo* 69c6 and *Republic* VII 533d1–2, while the talk of the death of the soul recalls the argument of *Phaedo* 102a10–107a1, as in Chapter 11; the final words of the chapter, "going to Hades and falling asleep there" are a quotation from *Republic* VII 534c7–d1. Plotinus uses similar language, recalling similar passages of Plato, in I.6.5, 39–45, I.6.6, 1–5 and VI.7.31, 25–27 (cf. also I.6.8, 11–16).

Chapter 14

In this chapter Plotinus considers yet another objection which locates the origin of evil in the soul, namely that vice is a "weakness" in the soul. In response he argues that such weakness comes not from the soul itself but from matter. He is thus led to give a more detailed account than before of the relationship between matter and soul and the way in which matter causes evil in the soul.

14, 1–7 The objection is expressed in terms which recall both the division of the soul into three parts found in Plato's *Republic*—a desiring part, a spirited part where emotions such as anger are located, and a reasoning part—and the epistemology of the Stoics, in which "assent" and "impressions" are key concepts. (For a brief account of Stoic epistemology, see Sharples [1996, 20–23] or, for a fuller discussion, Sellars [2006, 64–78].) Plato refers to moral evil as "weakness" in *Republic* IV 444d13–e2 (cf. also *Gorgias* 477b3–5). The Stoic Chrysippus described emotions as false judgements due to weak assent: see *SVF* III.172 and 548. Posidonius, whose philosophy combined Stoicism with elements of Platonism, criticized Chrysippus but continued to use the language of "weakness" (see fr.164 Edelstein-Kidd). Plotinus rejects any view which ascribes weakness to the soul without reference to matter. "Breaths of wind and the heat of the sun" are mentioned in Plato, *Republic* II 380e3–7 and Aristotle, *Physics* 2.5.197a23 as examples of external factors which can affect things in nature (cf. also Plato, *Republic* III 404b2).

14, 8 *the nature and . . . in the soul*: These words echo the title of the treatise and 1, 1–4; in accordance with what was said there, Plotinus here discusses the nature of evil in the soul before giving an account of its source.

14, 9–17 Plotinus will argue in this chapter that matter is the cause of weakness in the soul, as of weakness in bodies. He introduces the point already here, after briefly considering that the soul can be described as "weak" only by analogy with the body. The Stoics, as materialists, described passions in material terms as diseases of the soul (see, for example, *SVF* III.421 and Posidonius fr. 163). Plotinus takes a completely different view of the nature of the soul and is anxious to explain that talk of weakness in the soul should not be understood in physical terms.

14, 12–13 *unless the cause . . . same, namely matter*: The somewhat awkward flow of the argument in lines 9–17 has led to the suggestion that these words are a gloss (see Alekniene [2006]). However, given the importance to Plotinus of the conclusion that matter is the cause of weakness in the soul, I see no reason why he should not have already stated it here, before developing the argument of the chapter.

14, 17–24 In lines 10–11 weakness in bodies was described as "lack of ability to perform their function and being easily affected," and Plotinus went on to suggest that souls could be described as weak in an analogous way. Now he returns to the point already made in 4, 14–17, that only souls that have entered into matter can become evil and unable to perform their function; souls which are not in matter are pure and their function is unimpeded. The words "winged and perfect" come from Plato *Phaedrus* 246b7–c1, the mythical description of souls that have not yet fallen into bodies; the statement that the function of such souls is unimpeded recalls Plotinus' use of *Republic* I 352e–353e in Chapters 11 and 13 (see Commentary 11, 10–19 and Commentary 13, 1–2). At the end of this passage Plotinus prepares the reader for the account of matter's relationship to soul which will follow; weakness in fallen, impure souls is "the presence of something alien" (cf. 1.6.5, 46–50). Although he has denied that such weakness is to be seen as a disease, he is still willing to use an analogy with bodily disease, brought about by phlegm or bile, the humors mentioned in Plato, *Republic* VIII 564c1 and *Timaeus* 82e6–7 as causing disease in the body; their effects are described in some detail in *Timaeus* 85.

14, 25–37 Plotinus explains how he understands the relationship between matter and soul. Soul has no spatial location: when it is described as "separate" this means that it is not joined to matter; when it is in matter, then matter acts as a substrate, rather like the receptacle in Plato's *Timaeus,* which in 52a–b is described as the "space" (*chōra*) which provides a place (*topos*) in which the sensible world comes to be. The difficulty for Plotinus, here as elsewhere, is to explain how soul enters into matter. (Cf., for example, III.2.4, 36–44 and III.3.4, 44–50). In order to resist any suggestion that the origin of evil lies in the soul, he pushes as much of the responsibility onto matter as his overall philosophical position will allow. He sees matter as restricting the expression of the many powers of the soul (cf. II.9.2, 4–9), and to describe how matter behaves he borrows language from the story of Poros and Penia in Plato, *Symposium* 203b2–c1, just as he does in III.6.14, 5–26: like Penia (Poverty), matter comes begging and makes its way in where it does not belong. (Cf. the description of evil as "utter poverty" in 3, 16 and see Commentary 3, 12–16. See also Fleet [1995, 236–239].) Schäfer (2004, 273–274) suggests that the description of matter as "begging" and "importuning" reflects the point of view of the soul which "feels bothered by amorphous matter's simultaneous greed and incapacity for being." Matter is ultimately passive and is not an independent principle of evil; yet it affects the soul in a way which leads to evil. To show that he believes in the overall goodness of the universe, Plotinus describes it as suffused with soul and uses an approximate quotation from Sophocles, *Oedipus at Colonus* 54 to back up the point (cf. also *Oedipus at Colonus* 16).

14, 38–43 Plotinus retreats from the description of matter in lines 35–36, where it might have appeared to have something of an active role, and returns to the imagery of light used earlier in the treatise and in the fuller account of the embodied soul in 1.1, 7–8 and 12. The role ascribed to matter here is difficult to understand, not to say paradoxical: it seems that, just by being there, it weakens the soul and "offers it generation and the cause of coming into matter." Plotinus presents his view in metaphorical language; in more technical philosophical terms, we could say that for him matter is a necessary cause of evil in the soul, but not a sufficient one, and that in the following lines he attempts to explain more fully just how the presence of matter brings about evil in a fallen soul. (Cf. O'Brien [1971, 126], O'Brien [1996, 186–187].)

Translation of this passage presents a number of problems. The verb *labein* in line 39 could mean either "take"/"receive" or "understand;" I have rendered it by the similarly ambiguous "grasp" in English. Otherwise I have followed the interpretation and punctuation of O'Brien (1971, 135) and O'Meara (1999, 82–83n81); like them, I take the unexpressed subject of *horāi* ("it sees") in line 40 to be soul, the source of illumination, rather than matter.

14, 44–49 Plotinus expands on the point made in lines 40–43, once again using language borrowed from Plato's *Symposium*, this time from 206d6, where the presence of ugliness is said to cause a creature which is pregnant to contract, turn away and fail to give birth. As in lines 35–36, the language here could be read as giving matter something of an active role, but Schäfer (2000, 30n66) suggests that the ascription to matter of "a kind of theft," like the earlier description of matter as "begging" and "importuning," projects onto matter the soul's view of what is going on.

14, 49–54 Plotinus' metaphysics commits him to the view that matter is generated by soul, but here he declares that matter is evil before soul is, and that it is the presence of matter which brings about evil in the soul. There has been considerable scholarly discussion of this passage and its implications: See, in particular, O'Brien (1971, 135–139); Schwyzer (1973, 274–277); Rist (1974, 500–502); Corrigan (1986, 172–176); O'Meara (1993, 84–85); Narbonne (1993, 202–207); Narbonne (2006); Narbonne (2007); and Brisson (2014, 176–179 and 185–186). Two points of detail need to be considered before an overall interpretation of the lines can be reached. The first regards the interpretation of the conditional statement, ". . . even if the soul itself generated matter in being affected, and if it consorted with it and became evil, matter by its presence is the cause . . . " while the second concerns exactly what is meant by talk of the soul "being affected" (*pathousa*). I agree with O'Brien and others (e.g., Kalligas [2014, 240]) that the conditional formulation here does not imply that Plotinus is not committed to the view that the soul generates matter; III.9.3, 7–14 offers a similar account of the production of matter in which the soul, wishing to be directed towards itself, "makes an image of itself, the non-existent, as if walking on emptiness and becoming more indefinite." This is the experience to which "being affected" here refers. Once generated, matter, by its very indefiniteness, is evil and, as such, causes the weakness which is evil in the soul.

Plotinus' view here is subtle and complex. His aim is both to argue against any view that makes soul ultimately responsible for evil, and at the same time to avoid postulating matter as a separate, active principle of evil. This involves him in a very difficult balancing act, and it may be doubted whether he performs that successfully. For Proclus' criticisms of Plotinus on this issue, see Introduction 36–39.

Chapter 15

Plotinus begins this chapter by considering two more objections to his view that matter is the source of evil. The first, that matter does not exist, he deals with in very summary fashion by referring to his own discussion elsewhere. His response to the second objection is also quite brief: he argues that the claim that there is no such thing as evil implies that there is no such thing as good either, a position which he is not prepared to accept. He points out that the concepts of desire, avoidance, and intellection all imply the existence of some good, before reiterating his view that evil in the soul comes from something outside it. The second part of the chapter functions as a conclusion to the treatise as a whole. Here Plotinus uses language and ideas drawn from Plato's Philebus *to sketch an account of the mixture of good and evil in the world and of the psychology of the embodied soul. In his final paragraph he strikes an optimistic note, stressing the inferiority of evil as compared with good and reminding his readers that it is always possible for us to turn back towards the good.*

15, 1–3 Plotinus has already alluded in 11, 6–7 to "some arguments which claim to remove matter entirely," but he deals with this objection so briskly that it is not clear what form such arguments take. O'Meara (1999, 158) lists a number of possibilities: rejection of the specifically Plotinian understanding of matter; rejection of matter as a principle (*archē*); the view deriving from Aristotle that matter exists only potentially; and the view of matter as "utter non-being" rather than "something different from what is" (cf. 3–9). In II.4.6 Plotinus argues along Aristotelian lines that there must be something underlying body, while in III.6.14 he uses language and imagery from Plato's *Timaeus* and *Symposium* to argue that matter is a necessary precondition of the sensible world; in II.4.11–12 he responds to an objection to his own view of matter as without size. Both II.4 and III.6 precede I.8 in the chronological order of the *Enneads,* and Plotinus could be referring to both these discussions here. If he is referring specifically to II.4.11–12, then the objection may be the same as the one to which he responds there.

15, 3–9 The question whether evil exists in reality was raised at the very beginning of the treatise, in 1, 6. Plotinus has argued, in Chapter 2, that there is no evil in the intelligible world, and in Chapter 7 that nevertheless evil necessarily exists as matter. Now he offers a fresh argument for the existence of evil, that it is implied by the existence of good (cf. III.3.7, 2–3 and VI.7.23, 15–17), and by desire, avoidance, and intellection. We might be tempted to read lines 6–7 as making the point that the concepts of desire and avoidance imply the concepts of good and evil. However, Plotinus presents this in a much more objectivist way, saying that the *existence* of desire and avoidance implies the *existence* of good and evil.

15, 7–9 *intellection and wisdom . . . that are good*: Plotinus has already made clear in 9, 2–3 that he regards wisdom as a virtue (see Commentary 9, 2–3 and cf. also 1, 8). His phrasing here may reflect the specification of 'intellect and wisdom' (*nous kai phronēsis*) as pure and true forms of knowledge in Plato's *Philebus* (58d6–7, 59d1, 63c5–6, 65e4, 66b5–6), a dialogue which he has very much in mind in the next paragraph.

15, 9–12 For Plotinus the world in which we live is neither totally good nor totally evil, but a realm in which good and evil are mixed (cf. III.2.7 and III.3.6, 11–13). Before he returns once again to the question of evil in the soul, he gives a brief general account of this realm of mixture, using language reminiscent of the metaphysics of Plato's *Philebus* (see esp. *Philebus* 23c9–d1 and 24e7–25b6) as well as of the mixture of intellect and necessity in *Timaeus* 47e5–48a1, quoted in 7, 4–5.

15, 11–12 *makes its contribution to the totality of evil*: The manuscripts here read "*ekeinōi en tōi holōi kakon.*" I follow

$H\text{-}S_2$ in inserting the relative pronoun *ho* between *ekeinōi* and *en*, but have tried to translate the phrase in a way which avoids attributing to Plotinus a belief in a principle of absolute evil (cf. O'Brien [1993, 33n15]).

15, 12–23 Now Plotinus turns his, and our, attention back to the soul. Picking up the mention of desire in lines 5–7, he declares that desires (other than the desire for intellect), emotions, imagination, and false opinion are all the result of soul's contact with matter, returning to ideas already presented in Chapter 4. By "the composite" Plotinus means the compound of soul and body (cf. Blumenthal [1971, 20–21]). He offers a similar account of perception and emotion in I.1.5, 8–26 and I.1.7, 1–6 (cf. also IV.4.19, 1–12). Here he seems to have in mind the psychology of Plato's *Philebus* 31c2–39c6 where pleasure and pain, desire, fear, and false opinion are all analyzed as arising from the combination of soul and body.

15, 18–19 *Imagination comes from . . . is not partless*: In IV.3.31 Plotinus puts forward a theory of two "image-making powers," one which receives images of perceptible things and another which reflects images of the intelligible. In this passage, as in I.2.5, 21–24, III.6.4, 20–23, IV.4.28, 40–43 and VI.8.3, 11–21, he is talking only about the first of these two (cf. Blumenthal [1971, 88–95]).

15, 23–28 Plotinus ends the treatise on a positive note, using a striking comparison of the evil in the world to prisoners bound in chains of gold. Stories of tribes in Ethiopia that used chains of gold as fetters go back to Herodotus and were repeated by later Greek authors (see Herodotus 3.22.2, Dio Chrysostom, *On wealth* [79].3 and Heliodorus, *Aethiopica* 9.1.5; cf. Kalligas [2014, 240]). Plotinus might also be thinking of Sophocles, *Electra* 837–838 which alludes to Amphiaraus being hidden "by nets bound with gold," or, as Igal suggests, of Homer, *Iliad* 15.19–20, where Zeus reminds Hera of the time when he punished her by hanging her with anvils attached to her feet and her hands bound with an unbreakable golden chain. Just as Plato in the *Phaedo* (74b4–c10) and the *Phaedrus* (249e4–250c6) saw the physical world as reminding us, through sense-perception, of the world of Forms, so Plotinus notes that, even when we see evil in the world, we also see images of the beautiful, that is, reflections of Forms, which remind us of the intelligible (cf. I.6.3, III.5.1, 30–62 and V.3.2, 9–16). The description of evil as hidden by the fetters of form recalls the allusion in 9, 13 to ugliness being hidden (cf. also V.8.7, 21–22 where it is matter that is hidden under a multiplicity of forms).

15, 26 *so that, though present, matter may not be seen by the gods*: My translation here ("though present") accepts O'Meara's conjecture *hina parousa* for the puzzling *hina ousa* of the manuscripts and I follow him in taking *hē hylē*, "matter," as the implied subject of the feminine participle, *parousa*. He supports his conjecture by drawing attention to the references to matter as "present" in Chapter 14, lines 24, 34, 40 and 54. (See O'Meara [1999, 86n90 and 163]. He also cites 5, 30–31 and the remarks in 9, 18–26 on the difficulty of "seeing" matter.) Dodds (1965, 420) conjectured *hin'amousa* in view of the "aesthetico-moral context" of the passage and the use of *amousos* in Plato *Laws* IX 863c7 to describe the morally ugly; on this reading *amousa* would be neuter plural and the translation would be as in Armstrong (1989, 317): "so that it may not appear in its charmlessness to the gods."

Select Bibliography

I. Ancient Authors

ALCINOUS: *The Handbook of Platonism*, trans. and ed. Dillon, J. M. 1993. Oxford: Clarendon Press.

ALEXANDER OF APHRODISIAS: *Praeter Commentaria Scripta Minora*, ed. Bruns, I. 1887–1892. Berlin: G. Reimer.

Quaestiones 1.1–2.15, trans. Sharples, R.W. 1992. London: Duckworth.

Supplement to On the Soul, trans. Sharples, R. W. 2004. London: Duckworth.

De Anima Libri Mantissa, ed. Sharples, R.W. 2008. Berlin: De Gruyter.

ARISTOTLE: *Ethica Nicomachea*, ed. Bywater, I. 1894. Oxford: Clarendon Press.

De generatione et corruptione, ed. Joachim, H. H. 1922. Oxford: Clarendon Press.

Metaphysics, ed. Ross, W. D. 1924. Oxford: Clarendon Press.

De caelo, ed. Allan, D. J. 1936. Oxford: Clarendon Press.

Categoriae et Liber de interpretatione, ed. Minio-Paluello, L. 1949. Oxford: Clarendon Press.

Parts of Animals, ed. and trans. Peck, A. L. 1937. London: Heinemann (Loeb).

Prior and Posterior Analytics, ed. Ross, W. D. 1949. Oxford: Clarendon Press.

Topica et Sophistici Elenchi, ed. Ross, W. D. 1958. Oxford: Clarendon Press.

De anima, ed. Ross, W. D. 1961. Oxford: Clarendon Press

Physica, ed. Ross, W. D. 1966. Oxford. Clarendon Press.

The Complete Works: The Revised Oxford Translation, ed. Barnes, J. 1995. Princeton: Princeton University Press.

DIO CHRYSOSTOM, *Discourses 61–80*, trans. Crosby, H. L. 1951. London: Heinemann (Loeb).

DIOGENES LAERTIUS, *Lives of Eminent Philosophers*, trans. Hicks, R. D. 1925. London: Heinemann (Loeb).

GALEN: *Opera omnia*, ed. Kühn, C. G. 1964–1965. Hildesheim: G. Olms.

Psychological Writings, trans. and ed. Singer, P. N., Nutton, V. and Davies, D. 2013. Cambridge: Cambridge University Press.

Works on Human Nature, vol. 1, Mixtures (De temperamentis), trans. and ed. Singer, P. N. and van der Eijk, P. J. 2018. Cambridge. Cambridge University Press.

HELIODORUS, *Aethiopica*, ed. Bekker, I. 1855. Leipzig: Teubner.

Ethiopian Story, trans. Lamb, W. R. M., ed. Morgan, J. R. 1997. London: Everyman.

HERODOTUS, *The Persian Wars. Books 3–4*, trans. Godley, A. D. 1921. London: Heinemann (Loeb).

HOMER, *Iliad XIII-XXIV*, ed. Monro, D. B. and Allen, T. W. 3rd edn. 1920. Oxford: Clarendon Press.

HOMER, *Iliad*, trans. Fagles, R. 1990. New York: Viking Penguin.

NEMESIUS, *De natura hominis*, ed. Morani, M. 1987. Leipzig: Teubner.

On the Nature of Man, trans. Sharples, R. W. and van der Eijk, P. J. 2008. Liverpool: Liverpool University Press.

NUMENIUS: *Fragments*, ed. and trans. des Places, E. 1973. Paris: Les Belles Lettres.

ORIGEN: *Traité des principes*, ed. and trans. Crouzel, H. and Simonetti, M. 1978–1984. 5 vols. Paris: Cerf.

PLATO: *Opera*, ed. Burnet, J. 1902–1906. Oxford: Clarendon Press.

Complete Works, trans. Cooper, J. M. and Hutchinson, D. S. 1997. Indianapolis: Hackett.

Alcibiades, ed. Denyer, N. 2001. Cambridge: Cambridge University Press.

PLUTARCH: *Moralia XIII Parts I and 2*, ed. and trans. Cherniss, H. F. 1976. Cambridge, Mass: Heinemann (Loeb).

PORPHYRY, *Fragmenta*, ed. Smith, A. 1993. Stuttgart: Teubner.

Life of Plotinus in Loeb Plotinus, vol. 1, ed. and trans. Armstrong, A. H. 1969. Cambridge, MA: Harvard University Press.

POSIDONIUS, *Fragments*, ed. and trans. L. Edelstein and I. G. Kidd. 1989, 1999. 3 vols. Cambridge: Cambridge University Press.

PROCLUS: *In Platonis Rem publicam Commentarii*, ed. Kroll, W. 1899–1901. 2 vols. Leipzig: Teubner.

In Platonis Timaeum Commentaria, ed. Diehl, E. 1903–1906. 2 vols. Leipzig: Teubner.

Théologie platonicienne II, ed. and trans. Saffrey, H-D. and Westerink, L. G. 1974. Paris: Les Belles Lettres.

On the Existence of Evils, trans. Opsomer, J. and Steel, C. 2003. London: Duckworth.

Commentary on Plato's Timaeus, trans. Baltzly, D., Runia, D. T., Share, M. and Tarrant, H. 2007–2017. 6 vols. Cambridge: Cambridge University Press.

Ten Problems Concerning Providence, trans. Opsomer, J. and Steel, C. 2012. London: Bristol Classical Press.

Commentary on Plato's Republic, vol. I, trans. Baltzly, D., Finamore, J. F. and Miles, G. 2018. Cambridge: Cambridge University Press.

SIMPLICIUS, *In Aristotelis Categorias Commentarium*, ed. Kalbfleisch, C. 1907. Berlin: Reimer.

On Aristotle Categories 5-6, trans. de Haas, F. A. J. and Fleet, B. 2001. London: Duckworth.

SOPHOCLES, *Ajax, Electra, Oedipus Tyrannus,* trans. Lloyd-Jones, H. 1994. Cambridge, MA: Harvard University Press (Loeb).

Antigone, the Women of Trachis, Philoctetes, Oedipus at Colonus, trans. Lloyd-Jones, H. 1994. Cambridge, MA: Harvard University Press (Loeb).

Stoicum Veterum Fragmenta (*SVF*), ed. Von Arnim, H. 1905–1924. Leibzig: Teubner.

II. Editions and Translations of the Enneads

Armstrong, A. H. 1966–1982. *Plotinus, Enneads.* Greek Text with English Translation and Introductions. 7 vols. Cambridge, MA: Loeb.

———. 1989. *Plotinus, Enneads.* Greek Text with English Translation and Introductions. Vol. 1. Revised edn. Cambridge, MA: Loeb.

Atkinson, Michael. 1983. *Plotinus: Ennead V.1.* Greek Text with English Translation and Commentary. Oxford: Oxford University Press.

Bréhier, Émile. 1924–1938. *Plotin, Ennéades.* Greek Text and French Translation with Introductions and Notes. 7 vols. Paris: Les Belles Lettres.

Brisson, Luc and Jean François Pradeau, eds. 2002–2010. *Plotin, Traités.* French Translation and Introductions. 8 vols. Paris: Flammarion.

Cilento, Vincenzo. 1947–1949. *Plotino, Enneadi.* Italian Translation and Commentary. 3 vols. Bari: Laterza.

Creuzer, Georg Friedrich. 1835. *Plotini Enneades.* Greek Text, with Marsilio Ficino's Latin Translation and Commentary. Oxford: E Typographeo Academico.

Fleet, Barrie. 1995. *Plotinus. Ennead III.6.* Greek Text with English Translation and Commentary. Oxford: Clarendon Press.

Gerson L. P., ed. 2018. *Plotinus, The Enneads*. Trans. Cambridge: Cambridge University Press.

Harder, Richard, Beutler, Robert, and Theiler, Willy. 1956–1971. *Plotins Schriften*. Greek Text with German Translation and Commentary. 12 vols. Hamburg: Meiner.

Henry, Paul and Schwyzer, Hans-Rudolph. 1951–1973. *Plotini Opera* I-III (editio maior). Paris: Desclée de Brouwer et Cie (HS_1).

———. 1964–1982. *Plotini Opera* I-III (editio minor, with revised text). Oxford: Clarendon Press (HS_2).

———. 1973. *Addenda et Corrigenda ad textum et apparatum lectionum*. In HS_1, t. III (HS_3).

———. 1982. *Addenda et Corrigenda ad textum et apparatum lectionum*. In HS_2, t. III (HS_4).

Igal, Jesus. 1982–1998. *Plotino, Enéadas*. 3 vols. Introduction, translations and notes. Madrid: Gredos.

Kalligas, P. 1994-2018 *Plotinus Enneads* (text and commentary in modern Greek). 6 vols. Athens: Akademia Athinon.

———. 2014. *The Enneads of Plotinus: A Commentary*. Vol. 1. (English translation by E. K. Fowden and N. Pilavachi of the commentary published in modern Greek in 1994.) Princeton: Princeton University Press.

Kirchhoff, Adolph. 1856. *Plotini Opera*. Leipzig: Teubner.

Lavaud, Laurent. 2010. In *Plotin. Traités 51-54. Porphyre. Vie de Plotin*, eds. Brisson, L. and Pradeau, J-F. Paris: Flammarion.

Long, A. A. 2022. *Plotinus.* Ennead *II.4. On Matter.* English Translation with Introduction and Commentary. Las Vegas: Parmenides Publishing.

MacKenna, Stephen. 1962[3]. *Plotinus: The Enneads.* English Translation. Revised by B. S. Page. London: Faber & Faber.

———. 1991. *Plotinus. The Enneads.* Selected Treatises Revised with Notes by John Dillon. London: Penguin.

O'Meara, Dominic J. 1999. *Plotin. Traité 51 (I.8): introduction, traduction, commentaires et notes.* Paris: Les Editions du Cerf.

Schwyzer, Hans-Rudolph. 1987. "Corrigenda ad Plotini Textum." *Museum Helveticum* 44, 181–210 (HS_5).

Ueng, Jia-Sheng. 1993. *Plotinus on Matter and Evil: a commentary on Plotinus'* Enneads *1.8 "On What Are and Whence Come Evils?"* PhD dissertation. Liverpool.

III. Studies on I.8 and Related Works

Alekniene, Tatjana. 2006. "Une glose dans le *traité* 51 [I,8]. 14, 12–13 de Plotin?" *Philologus* 150:177–178.

Beierwaltes, Werner. 1977. "Plotins Metaphysik des Lichtes." In Zintzen (1977, 75–117). Originally published in *Zeitschrift für Philosophische Forschung* XV (1961): 334–362.

———. 1985. *Denken des Einen: Studien zur neuplatonischen Philosophie und ihrer Wirkungsgeschichte.* Frankfurt am Main: V. Klostermann.

Blumenthal, Henry J. 1971. *Plotinus' Psychology: His Doctrines of the Embodied Soul.* The Hague: Martinus Nijhoff.

———. 1993. "Plotinus and Proclus on the Criterion of Truth." Essay IX in *Soul and Intellect. Studies in Plotinus and Later Neoplatonism.* Aldershot: Variorum (Ashgate). Originally published in *The Criterion of Truth*, edited by Pamela Huby and Gordon Neal, 257–280. 1989. Liverpool: Liverpool University Press, 257–280.

Bonazzi, Mauro. 2007. "Eudorus of Alexandria and Early Imperial Platonism." In *Greek Philosophy 100 BC – 200 AD*, Vol. II, edited by Robert W. Sharples and Richard Sorabji, 365–377. London: University of London, School of Advanced Study, Institute of Classical Studies.

Boys-Stones, George. 2018. *Platonist Philosophers 80 BC to AD 250.* Cambridge: Cambridge University Press.

Brisson, Luc. 2014. "The Question of Evil in the World of Plotinus." In *Fate, Providence and Moral Responsibility in Ancient, Medieval and Early Modern Thought*, edited by Pieter d'Hoine and Gerd Van Riel, 171–186. Leuven: Leuven University Press.

Clark, Stephen R. L. 2016. *Plotinus: Myth, Metaphor, and Philosophical Practice.* Chicago: The University of Chicago Press.

Corrigan, Kevin. 1986. "Is there more than one generation of matter in the *Enneads*?" *Phronesis* 31: 167–181.

———. 1996a. "Essence and Existence in the *Enneads.*" In Gerson (1996, 105–129).

———. 1996b. *Plotinus' Theory of Matter-Evil and the Question of Substance: Plato, Aristotle, and Alexander of Aphrodisias.* Leuven: Peeters.

Dodds, E. R. 1965. "Review of *Plotini Opera*, ed. P. Henry and H-R. Schwyzer [Ed. Minor], T. I." *Gnomon* 37: 419–420.

Dörrie, Heinrich. 1970. "Der König. Ein platonisches Schlüsselwort, von Plotin mit neuem Sinn erfüllt." *Revue internationale de philosophie* 24: 217–235. Reprinted in *Platonica Minora*, 1976. Munich: W. Fink. 390–405.

Festugière, André-Jean. 1949–1954. *La Révélation d'Hermès Trismégiste.* 3 vols. Paris: Lecoffre.

Hadot, Pierre. 1960. "Etre, Vie, Pensée chez Plotin et avant Plotin." In *Les sources de Plotin (Entretiens Hardt V)*. Fondation Hardt: Geneva, 105–141.

Hager, F. P. 1977. "Die Materie und das Böse im antiken Platonismus." In Zintzen (1977, 427–474). Originally published in *Museum Helveticum* 19 (1962) 73–103.

Igal, Jesús. 1977. "Observaciones a las Ennéadas I–II de Plotino: texto y fuentes." *Helmantica* 28: 241–252.

Karamanolis, George. 2006. *Plato and Aristotle in Agreement? Platonists on Aristotle from Antiochus to Porphyry*. Oxford: Clarendon Press.

Long, A. A. 2016. "What is the Matter with Matter According to Plotinus?" *Royal Institute of Philosophy Supplement* 78: 37–54.

Meijer, P. A. 1992. *Plotinus on the Good or the One (Enneads VI.9): An Analytical Commentary*. Amsterdam: J. C. Gieben.

Narbonne, Jean-Marc. 1993. *Plotin. Les deux matières: Ennéade II.4 (12); introduction, texte grec, traduction et commentaire*. Paris: J. Vrin

———. 2001. *La métaphysique de Plotin*. 2nd edn. Paris: J. Vrin.

———. 2006. "Plotinus and the Gnostics on the Generation of Matter (33 [II 9], 12 and 51 [I 8], 14)." *Dionysius* 24: 45–64.

———. 2007. "A Doctrinal Evolution in Plotinus? The Weakness of the Soul in its Relation to Evil." *Dionysius* 25: 77–92.

O'Brien, Denis. 1971. "Plotinus on Evil. A study of matter and the soul in Plotinus' conception of human evil." In *Le néoplatonisme* (Colloque international du CNRS) Paris: Editions du CNRS, 113–46.

———. 1977. "Le volontaire et la nécessité: réflexions sur la descente de l'âme dans la philosophie de Plotin." *Revue philosophique de la France et de l'étranger* 167: 401–422.

———. 1992. "Origène et Plotin sur le roi de l'univers." In ΣΟΦΙΗΣ ΜΑΙΗΤΟΡΕΣ. *"Chercheurs de sagesse." Hommage à Jean Pépin.* Edited by Marie-Odile Goulet-Cazé, Goulven Madec, and Denis O'Brien, 317–342. Paris: Etudes Augustiniennes.

———. 1993. *Théodicée plotinienne, théodicée gnostique.* Leiden: Brill.

———. 1996. "Plotinus on Matter and Evil." In Gerson (1996, 171–195).

———. 2012. "Plotinus on the Making of Matter Part III: The Essential Background." *International Journal of the Platonic Tradition* 6: 27–80.

O'Meara, Dominic J. 1998. "Evil in Plotinus (*Enn.* I 8)." In *The Structure of Being and the Search for Good*, Aldershot: Variorum, Essay IX.

———. 2005. "The Metaphysics of Evil in Plotinus: Problems and Solutions." In *Agonistes: Essays in Honour of Denis O'Brien*, edited by John Dillon and Monique Dixsaut, 179–185. Aldershot: Ashgate, 179–185.

Opsomer, Jan. 2001. "Proclus vs. Plotinus on Matter (*De mal. Subs.* 30–7)." *Phronesis* 46: 154–188.

———. 2022. "Matter and Evil." In Gerson and Wilberding (2022, 341–62).

Pépin. Jean. 1971. *Idées grecques sur l'homme et sur dieu.* Paris: Les Belles Lettres.

Rist, John M. 1974. "Plotinus and Augustine on Evil." In *Plotino e il Neoplatonismo in Oriente e in Occidente*, 495–508. Rome: Accademia Nazionale dei Lincei.

Schäfer, Christian. 2000. "Das Dilemma der neuplatonischen Theodizee: Versuch einer Lösung." *Archiv für Geschichte der Philosophie* 82: 1–35.

———. 2004. "Matter in Plotinus' Normative Ontology." *Phronesis* 49: 266–294.

Schwyzer, Hans-Rudolf. 1973. "Zu Plotins Deutung der sogenannten platonischen Materie." In *Zetesis* (Festschrift E. de Strycker), 266–280. Antwerp: De Nederlandsche Boekhandel.

Sellars, John. 2006. ***Stoicism.*** Chesham: Acumen.

Sharples, Robert W. 1994. "Plato, Plotinus and Evil." *Bulletin of the Institute of Classical Studies* 39: 171–181.

———. 1996. *Stoics, Epicureans and Sceptics.* London: Routledge.

Sheppard, Anne. 2020. "Plotinus on Choral Dancing." *Classics Ireland* 27: 98–109.

Sleeman, J. H. 1926. "Some Notes on Plotinus." *Classical Quarterly* 20: 152–154.

———. 1937. "Harder's Plotinus." *Classical Review* 51: 225–226.

Stern-Gillet, Suzanne. 2019. "Ὁμοίωσις θεῷ in the *Theaetetus* and in Plotinus." *Ancient Philosophy* 39: 89–117.

Zintzen, Clemens, ed. 1977. *Die Philosophie des Neuplatonismus.* Darmstadt: Wissenschaftliche Buchgesellschaft.

IV. General Publications

Armstrong, A. H. 1940. *The Architecture of the Intelligible Universe in the Philosophy of Plotinus.* Cambridge: Cambridge University Press.

Arnou, R. 1968. *Le Désir de Dieu dans la philosophie de Plotin.* 2nd ed. Rome: Presses de l'Université Grégorienne.

Dillon, J. 1977/1996. *The Middle Platonists: A Study of Platonism, 80 B.C.–A.D. 220,* London: Duckworth, 1977, 1996[2].

Dodds, Eric R. 1965. *Pagan and Christian in an Age of Anxiety: Some Aspects of Religious Experience from Marcus Aurelius to Constantine.* Cambridge: Cambridge University Press.

Emilsson, E. K. 1988. *Plotinus on Sense-Perception.* Cambridge: Cambridge University Press.

———. 2007. *Plotinus on Intellect.* Oxford: Clarendon Press.

———. 2017. *Plotinus.* London: Routledge.

Gerson, L. P. 1994. *Plotinus.* London/New York: Routledge.

———, ed. 1996. *The Cambridge Companion to Plotinus.* Cambridge: Cambridge University Press.

———, ed. 2010. *The Cambridge History of Philosophy in Late Antiquity.* 2 vols. Cambridge: Cambridge University Press.

Gerson, L. P. and Wilberding, J., eds. 2022. *The New Cambridge Companion to Plotinus.* Cambridge: Cambridge University Press.

Hadot, Pierre. 1993. *Plotinus on the Simplicity of Vision.* Translated by M. Chase. Chicago: Chicago University Press.

Inge, W. R. 1948. *The Philosophy of Plotinus.* 3rd ed. London: Longmans, Green.

Lloyd, Anthony C. 1990. *The Anatomy of Neoplatonism.* Oxford: Clarendon Press.

O'Daly, G. 1973. *Plotinus' Philosophy of the Self.* Shannon: Irish University Press.

O'Meara, Dominic J. 1993. *Plotinus: an Introduction to the Enneads.* Oxford: Oxford University Press.

Remes, Pauliina. 2008. *Neoplatonism.* Berkeley: University of California Press.

Remes, Pauliina and Slaveva-Griffin, Svetla, eds. 2014. *The Routledge Handbook of Neoplatonism.* London: Routledge.

Rist, John M. 1967. *Plotinus: The Road to Reality.* Cambridge: Cambridge University Press.

Schniewind, Alexandrine. 2003. *L'Éthique du Sage chez Plotin.* Paris: J. Vrin.

Smith, Andrew. 2004. *Philosophy in Late Antiquity.* London: Routledge.

Wallis, R. T. 1995. *Neoplatonism.* 2nd ed. London: Duckworth.

Index of Ancient Authors

Index of Names and Subjects

PRE-SOCRATICS

By Being, It Is: *The Thesis of Parmenides* by Néstor-Luis Cordero

The Fragments of *Parmenides*: *A Critical Text with Introduction and Translation, the Ancient Testimonia and a Commentary by A. H. Coxon. Revised and Expanded Edition edited with new Translations by Richard McKirahan and a new Preface* by Malcolm Schofield

The Legacy of Parmenides: *Eleatic Monism and Later Presocratic Thought* by Patricia Curd

Parmenides and the History of Dialectic: *Three Essays* by Scott Austin

Parmenides, Venerable and Awesome: *Proceedings of the International Symposium* edited by Néstor-Luis Cordero

Presocratics and Plato: *A Festschrift in Honor of Charles Kahn* edited by Richard Patterson, Vassilis Karasmanis, and Arnold Hermann

The Route of Parmenides: *Revised and Expanded Edition, With a New Introduction, Three Supplemental Essays, and an Essay* by Gregory Vlastos by Alexander P. D. Mourelatos

To Think Like God: *Pythagoras and Parmenides. The Origins of Philosophy. Scholarly and fully annotated edition* by Arnold Hermann

The Illustrated To Think Like God: *Pythagoras and Parmenides. The Origins of Philosophy* by Arnold Hermann (with over 200 full color illustrations)

PLATO

The Second Alcibiades: *A Platonist Dialogue on Prayer and on Ignorance* by Harold Tarrant

A Stranger's Knowledge: *Statesmanship, Philosophy, and Law in Plato's Statesman* by Xavier Márquez

God and Forms in Plato by Richard D. Mohr

Image and Paradigm in Plato's Sophist by David Ambuel

Imperial Plato: Albinus, Maximus, Apuleius by Ryan Fowler

Interpreting Plato's Dialogues by J. Angelo Corlett

One Book, the Whole Universe: *Plato's Timaeus Today* edited by Richard D. Mohr and Barbara M. Sattler

Platonic Patterns: *A Collection of Studies* by Holger Thesleff

Plato's Late Ontology: *A Riddle Resolved* by Kenneth M. Sayre

Plato's *Parmenides*: *Text, Translation & Introductory Essay* by Arnold Hermann. Translation in collaboration with Sylvana Chrysakopoulou with a Foreword by Douglas Hedley

Plato's Universe by Gregory Vlastos

ARISTOTLE

Aristotle's Empiricism: Experience and Mechanics in the Fourth Century B.C. by Jean De Groot

One and Many in Aristotle's Metaphysics—*Volume I: Books Alpha-Delta* by Edward C. Halper

One and Many in Aristotle's Metaphysics—*Volume 2: The Central Books* by Edward C. Halper

Reading Aristotle: Physics VII.3 "What is Alteration?" *Proceedings of the International ESAP-HYELE Conference* edited by Stefano Maso, Carlo Natali, and Gerhard Seel

HELLENISTIC PHILOSOPHY

A Life Worthy of the Gods: *The Materialist Psychology of Epicurus* by David Konstan

THE *ENNEADS* OF PLOTINUS

Translations with Introductions & Philosophical Commentaries
Series edited by John M. Dillon and Andrew Smith

Ennead* I.1: *What Is the Living Thing? What Is Man? by Gerard O'Daly

Ennead* I.5: *On Whether Well-Being Increases with Time by Danielle A. Layne

Ennead* I.6: *On Beauty by Andrew Smith

Ennead* II.5: *On What Is Potentially and What Actually by Cinzia Arruzza

Ennead* II.9: *Against the Gnostics by Sebastian Ramon Philipp Gertz

Ennead* II.4: *On Matter by; Anthony A. Long

Ennead* III.4: *On Our Allotted Guardian Spirit by Wiebke-Marie Stock

Ennead* IV.3–IV.4.29: *Problems concerning the Soul by John M. Dillon and H. J. Blumenthal

Ennead* IV.4.30–45 & IV.5: *Problems concerning the Soul by Gary M. Gurtler

Ennead IV.7: *On the Immortality of the Soul* by Barrie Fleet

Ennead* IV.8: *On the Descent of the Soul into Bodies by Barrie Fleet

Ennead* V.1: *On the Three Primary Levels of Reality by Eric D. Perl

Ennead* V.5: *That the Intelligibles are not External to the Intellect, and on the Good by Lloyd P. Gerson

Ennead* V.8: *On Intelligible Beauty by Andrew Smith

Ennead* VI.4 & VI.5: *On the Presence of Being, One and the Same, Everywhere as a Whole by Eyjólfur Emilsson and Steven Strange

Ennead* VI.8: *On the Voluntary and on the Free Will of the One by Kevin Corrigan and John D. Turner

ETHICS

Sentience and Sensibility: *A Conversation about Moral Philosophy* by Matthew R. Silliman

PHILOSOPHICAL FICTION

Pythagorean Crimes by Tefcros Michaelides

The Aristotle Quest: A Dana McCarter Trilogy. Book 1: Black Market Truth by Sharon M. Kaye

AUDIOBOOKS

The Iliad (unabridged) by Stanley Lombardo

The Odyssey (unabridged) by Stanley Lombardo

The Essential Homer by Stanley Lombardo

The Essential Iliad by Stanley Lombardo

FORTHCOMING

Ennead **I.2:** ***On Virtues*** by Suzanne Stern-Gillet

Ennead **I.3:** ***On Dialectic*** by Pauliina Remes

Ennead **I.4:** ***On Well-Being*** by Kieran McGroarty

Ennead **I.9:** ***On Going Out of the Body*** by Suzanne Stern-Gilet

Ennead **II.1:** ***On the Heavens by*** Andrew Smith

Ennead **II.6:** ***On Substance, or On Quality*** by Damien Caluori

Ennead **II.7:** ***On Complete Blending*** by Robert Goulding

Ennead **II.8:** ***On Sight*** by Robert Goulding

Ennead **III.5:** ***On Love*** by Sara Magrin

Ennead **III.6:** ***On Impassibility*** by Eleni Perdikouri

Ennead **III.7:** ***On Eternity and Time*** by László Bene

Ennead **III.8:** ***On Nature and Contemplation*** by George Karamanolis

Ennead **IV.6:** ***On Sense-Perception and Memory*** by Peter Lautner

Ennead **IV.9:** ***On Whether All Souls are One*** by Eyjólfur Emilsson

Ennead **V.2, V.4, and V.6:** ***On the One and Intellect*** by Eleni Perdikouri

Ennead **V.3:** ***On the Knowing Hypostases*** by Marie-Élise Zovko

Ennead **V.9:** ***On Intellect, Ideas, and Being*** by Matthias Vorwerk

Ennead **VI.1-2:** ***On the Genera of Being (I+II)*** by Damien Caluori and Regina Füchslin

Ennead **VI.3:** ***On the Genera of Being (III)*** by Riccardo Chiaradonna

Ennead **VI.7:** ***The Forms and the Good*** by Nicholas Banner